Human Resources

NATIONAL BUREAU OF ECONOMIC RESEARCH
General Series 96

Economic Research: Retrospect and Prospect

HUMAN RESOURCES

Fiftieth Anniversary Colloquium VI

NATIONAL BUREAU OF ECONOMIC RESEARCH

NEW YORK 1972

Distributed by COLUMBIA UNIVERSITY PRESS

NEW YORK AND LONDON

Relation of National Bureau Directors to Publications
Reporting Proceedings of the Fiftieth Anniversary Colloquia

Since the present volume is a record of colloquium proceedings, it has
been exempted from the rules governing submission of manuscripts to,
and critical review by, the Board of Directors of the National Bureau.
*(Resolution adopted July 6, 1948, as revised
November 21, 1949, and April 20, 1968)*

Prefatory Note

This volume of the Fiftieth Anniversary Series contains the proceedings of the Human Resources Colloquium, which was held on the campus of Clark College, Atlanta University, Atlanta, Georgia on May 13, 1971. We are indebted to those members of the Bureau's Board of Directors who served on the committee to plan and coordinate the session: Charles H. Berry, Wallace J. Campbell, Eugene P. Foley, Marion B. Folsom (currently not a Board member), Eli Goldston, Vivian W. Henderson, Harry W. Laidler (deceased), J. Irwin Miller, Boris Shishkin, and Lazare Teper. We wish to acknowledge, too, the splendid cooperation of the faculty of the Department of Economics at Clark College, who contributed substantial time and effort to ensuring the success of the Human Resources Colloquium. Finally, we are grateful to Ester Moskowitz, Hedy D. Jellinek, and Ruth Ridler, who prepared the manuscript for publication.

GARY S. BECKER

Fiftieth Anniversary Colloquium Series

To commemorate its fiftieth anniversary the National Bureau of Economic Research sponsored a series of colloquia to explore the effects of pending and anticipated policy issues on future research priorities for areas of long-standing Bureau concern. As a basis for the panel and audience discussions, economists specializing in the subject area prepared papers in which they reviewed relevant research advances through time and presented their opinions for the direction of future effort. These papers, and in some instances edited transcripts of panelists' comments, appear as part of the National Bureau's Fiftieth Anniversary publications series. Papers developed for the colloquia and publications series and participants in the program included:

THE BUSINESS CYCLE TODAY
September 24, 1970—New York City

Moderators:
Morning session: Paul A. Samuelson
Afternoon session: F. Thomas Juster

Presentations:
"Dating American Growth Cycles" *Ilse Mintz*
"The 'Recession' of 1969–1970" *Solomon Fabricant*
"The Cyclical Behavior of Prices" *Geoffrey H. Moore*
"Forecasting Economic Conditions: The Record and the Prospect"
Victor Zarnowitz
"Econometric Model Simulations and the Cyclical Characteristics of the U.S. Economy" *Victor Zarnowitz*
"A Study of Discretionary and Nondiscretionary Monetary and Fiscal Policies in the Context of Stochastic Macroeconometric Models" *Yoel Haitovsky and Neil Wallace*

Panelists:
 Morning session: Otto Eckstein, Henry C. Wallich
 Afternoon session: Bert G. Hickman, Arthur M. Okun

FINANCE AND CAPITAL MARKETS
October 22, 1970—New York City

Moderator: Robert V. Roosa

Presentation:
 "Finance and Capital Markets"   *John Lintner*

Panelists: William J. Baumol, Sidney Homer, James J. O'Leary

A ROUNDTABLE ON POLICY ISSUES AND RESEARCH OPPORTUNITIES IN INDUSTRIAL ORGANIZATION
November 5, 1970—Chicago, Illinois

Moderator: Victor R. Fuchs

Presentations:
 "Industrial Organization: Boxing the Compass"
               James W. McKie
 "Antitrust Enforcement and the Modern Corporation"
             Oliver E. Williamson
 "Issues in the Study of Industrial Organization in a Regime of Rapid
  Technical Change"   *Richard R. Nelson*
 "Industrial Organization: A Proposal for Research"
              Ronald H. Coase

PUBLIC EXPENDITURES AND TAXATION
December 2, 1970—Washington, D.C.

Moderator: Walter W. Heller

Presentation:
"Quantitative Research in Taxation and Government Expenditure"
Carl S. Shoup

Panelists: James M. Buchanan, Richard R. Musgrave

ECONOMIC GROWTH
December 10, 1970—San Francisco, California

Moderator: R. Aaron Gordon

Presentation:
"Is Growth Obsolete?"
William D. Nordhaus and James Tobin

Panelists: Moses Abramovitz, Robin C. O. Matthews

HUMAN RESOURCES
May 13, 1971—Atlanta, Georgia

Moderator: Gary S. Becker

Presentation:
"Human Capital: Policy Issues and Research Opportunities"
Theodore W. Schultz

Panelists: Alice M. Rivlin, Gerald S. Somers

THE FUTURE OF ECONOMIC RESEARCH
April 23, 1971—South Brookline, Massachusetts

Presentation:
  "Quantitative Economic Research: Trends and Problems"
Simon Kuznets

Contents

Foreword

Economists have been aware of the effects of education and training on earnings and productivity ever since Adam Smith's comment that "a man educated at the expence of much labour and time to any of those employments which require extraordinary dexterity and skill may be compared to one of those expensive machines. The work which he learns to perform, it must be expected, over and above the usual wages of common labour, will replace to him the whole expence of his education, with at least the ordinary profits of an equally valuable capital." [1] We need only note here the statements by McCulloch, that "man himself should . . . be considered as forming a part of the national capital"; [2] of Marshall, that "the most valuable of all capital is that invested in human beings"; [3] and of Fisher, that "the 'skill' of a mechanic is not wealth in addition to the man himself; it is the 'skilled mechanic' who should be put in the category of wealth." [4]

Yet, prior to the mid-fifties this awareness was not used to develop a major tool of analysis.[5] Investment in human beings was largely ignored in the discussions of economic growth, labor incomes, inequality in personal income distribution, international comparative advantage and specialization, savings and investment, unemployment and job turnover, or consumer expenditure patterns.

All this changed dramatically in the fifties, stimulated largely by a few puzzles and paradoxes that, as Schultz rightly emphasizes, contribute so much to advances in economic thinking. Studies largely at the National Bureau [6] showed that the growth in labor and capital as con-

[1] *Wealth of Nations*, p. 101, Modern Library Edition. Of course, Petty's calculations of the money value of a human being preceded Smith's work.

[2] See his *The Principles of Political Economy*, Alex Murray & Son, 1970, p. 66. I owe this reference to B. F. Kiker's "The Historical Roots of the Concept of Human Capital," *Journal of Political Economy*, October 1966.

[3] See his *Principles of Economics*, Macmillan and Co., 1938, p. 564.

[4] See his *The Nature of Capital and Income*, Macmillan and Co., 1930, p. 9.

[5] The one exception is the important study by Milton Friedman and Simon Kuznets *Income from Independent Professional Practice*, NBER, 1945.

[6] See, for example, Moses Abramovitz, *Resources and Output Trends in the United States Since 1870*, NBER, 1956.

ventionally measured failed dismally in explaining the growth in per capita incomes during the twentieth century in the United States. Or, contrary to expectations from factor-endowment trade theory, the United States apparently exports labor-intensive and imports capital-intensive goods.[7] A giant, yet in retrospect obvious, step in resolving both puzzles was the recognition that labor cannot be measured simply by man-hours since trained persons are more productive than other persons. Thus, the United States exports goods that use relatively large amounts of *skilled* labor, and the true labor input in the United States grew much faster than man-hours because investment in education and other training grew rapidly.

In the last fifteen years the analysis of investment in human capital has developed from these modest beginnings into a major field of study responsible for a significant breakthrough in our understanding of economic behavior. Its vitality is attested to by more than 1,000 entries in Blaug's bibliography of writings on the economics of education alone, by the prominence of economists in the National Academy of Education (chartered in 1965), by the proliferation of courses and research centers, by the demand for new Ph.D.'s with this specialty, by chapters in the annual reports of the Council of Economic Advisers, and by recognition from quarters initially hostile.

Any field that develops so rapidly is bound to take on trappings of a fad since much of the work is necessarily mechanical, repetitive, and of embarrassingly low quality. The analysis of investment in human capital has certainly had these trappings, and some critics are patiently waiting for the balloon to burst. Although periods of digestion and slow advance are inevitable, I am confident that this field will continue to grow rather than diminish in importance. My confidence results from the close ties of the kind already mentioned between theoretical developments and discussion, and empirical data and problems. This intimate relation of theory and observation has built a solid foundation that cannot easily be torn down or ignored.

What about future developments? Schultz gives an excellent discussion of the demand and supply considerations that determine the course of any economic research. He also offers a wide-ranging and insightful set of research opportunities on human capital provided by public and private demands for information, unsolved economic puzzles,

---

[7] See Wassily Leontief, "Factor Proportions and the Structure of American Trade: Further Theoretical and Empirical Analysis," *Review of Economics and Statistics,* 38, 1956, p. 386.

and advances in economic theory and empirical work. My own crystal ball says that the major breakthrough during the next decade will come in the application of human capital analysis to behavior in the nonmarket sector, an application also stressed by Schultz.

Practically all studies of the effects of investment in human capital have dealt with earnings, unemployment, occupation choice, and similar market decisions. Yet, education, for example, also affects whom one marries, the number of one's children and the amount invested in each child, labor force participation, health, expenditure patterns on goods and services, whether and how one votes, and many other dimensions of nonmarket behavior. Recent developments in the theory of the allocation of time and household production functions provide the tools for a rigorous analysis of the effects of human capital in the nonmarket sector. Before this decade is over we will have, I venture to guess, reliable and valuable estimates of the effects of human capital on nonmarket rates of return and productivity, and of the variety of changes in household decisions and expenditures of time and goods that are induced by a change in human capital.

GARY S. BECKER
The University of Chicago

Acknowledgments

John R. Meyer arranged for a small group to convene with me at the meetings of the directors of the National Bureau, September 20, 1969, to consider the objectives and scope of the proposed survey. Gary Becker served as chairman of this group. In doing the survey, I drew heavily upon my work that had been made possible by the generous grants of the Ford Foundation and upon the Ph.D. research of students supported by generous training grants in the area of human capital provided by the National Institute of Mental Health. It will be evident to the reader that I was privileged in having access to numerous as yet unpublished papers in the area of human capital. I owe a special debt to colleagues who critically reviewed early drafts of this survey: Gary S. Becker, Mary Jean Bowman, Samuel Bowles, Barry R. Chiswick, Richard B. Freeman, Zvi Griliches, W. Lee Hansen, Harry G. Johnson, Simon Kuznets, Jacob Mincer, Marc Nerlove, Yoram Ben-Porath, T. Paul Schultz, George J. Stigler, Luther G. Tweeten, Burton A. Weisbrod, and Finis Welch.

May 13, the day at Atlanta sponsored by the National Bureau to "test" the product, came off well indeed. I profited professionally from the presentations of the two panelists, Alice Rivlin and Gerald Somers, and from the incisive comments by members of the large group in attendance. Gary Becker presided and also entered actively into the discussions.

Nancy Steinthal of the NBER as "entrepreneur" and my secretary, Susan Gallager, as "translator" of what I wrote did much to make my task a pleasure. In preparing the bibliography I was assisted by Virginia Thurner.

THEODORE W. SCHULTZ
The University of Chicago

Human Resources

Human Capital: Policy Issues and Research Opportunities

Theodore W. Schultz
The University of Chicago

Human capital is a new research area in economics. It was the unexplained rise in the economic value of man that led to the concept of human capital. Extensions of investment theory to analyze the formation of human capital set the stage for empirical studies of a wide array of such investments. Then, seeing the associated rise in the value of time of human agents, this led to the further extension of economic theory to cope with the allocation of time, a development that has greatly increased the possibilities of analyzing nonmarket activities with special reference to the economic activities of the household. Human capital research has important policy implications, as I shall show.

My purpose in this survey is to examine some of the interactions between policy and research with special reference to human capital. As I proceed, I shall attempt to appraise the more important parts of this research—with a view to assessing the need for additional work in this area that may be useful in making policy decisions.[1] In thinking about these interactions, I find it helpful to approach them in terms of the supply of and demand for economic information. It is the intercept of the supply of this research and of the demand for it that should reveal the research opportunities. In short, then, the central purpose of my endeavor is to winnow the research opportunities in the area of human capital. Ideally, I would like to identify these opportunities and rate them in accordance with the potential value of their contributions to private and public decisions. But I shall settle for less because of the limitations of my knowledge and because of the uncertainty of the nature of the advances in knowledge that can be achieved by means of research.

[1] In the language of John R. Meyer in issuing the invitation that I undertake this task, it is "to appraise past research efforts in the (human capital) area of particular Bureau interest and involvement, and speculate about future undertakings . . . in light of present and future policy issues."

I shall begin with the setting and scope of the survey, and then turn to some of the supply-demand considerations underlying economic research that are also applicable to the area of human capital. Lastly, and most importantly, I shall enter upon the research opportunities in substantial detail.

I. SETTING AND SCOPE

The advances in human capital are of two basic parts. The "capital" part rests on the proposition that certain types of expenditure (sacrifices) create productive stocks embodied in man that provide services over future periods. The other part rests on the allocation of "time," which has led to the economic treatment of a wide array of nonmarket activities.

The linkage between these two parts is close and strong. The discovery of human capital in the growth context revealed the importance of earnings foregone in the formation of human capital. The development of micro theory extending the concept of earnings foregone led to the formulation of the theory of the allocation of time. This extension with special reference to micro theory of the household opened a new frontier in analyzing nonmarket activities.

The area of human capital rests predominantly upon the theoretical and empirical work of the last decade. It is, accordingly, a new area that has been developing rapidly, judging from the literally hundreds of professional papers and monographs that have appeared during the sixties.[2] It already has the earmarks of a major extension of economics. However, at this early date, it is doubtful whether anyone could present a truly complete and comprehensive appraisal of all of these developments and their implications for future research in view of the many studies at hand and in view of the difficulty of seeing them with enough perspective to distinguish between the transitory and permanent parts of this work.

A strong case can be made for using a rigorous definition of human capital in determining the scope of this survey. Such a definition will be formulated presently and will be useful up to a point, but it will be subject to the same ambiguities that continue to plague capital theory in general and the capital concept in economic growth models in particular.

---

[2] In the area of the economics of education alone, Mark Blaug's *Economics of Education: A Selected Annotated Bibliography,* London, Pergamon Press, 1966, includes 792 items, of which only eleven pertain to "earlier views." Professor Blaug has made available since then three addenda, bringing the number of items up to 1,183. The Pergamon Press published a new, up-to-date edition in 1971.

Capital is two-faced, and what these two faces tell us about economic growth, which is a dynamic process, are, as a rule, inconsistent stories. It must be so because the cost story is a tale about sunk investments, and the other story pertains to the discounted value of the stream of services that such capital renders, which changes with the shifting sands of growth. But worse still is the capital homogeneity assumption underlying capital theory and the aggregation of capital in growth models. As Hicks has taught us, the capital homogeneity assumption is the disaster of capital theory.[3] This assumption is demonstrably inappropriate in analyzing the dynamics of economic growth that is afloat on capital inequalities because of the differences in the rates of return, whether the capital aggregation is in terms of factor costs or in terms of the discounted value of the lifetime services of its many parts. Nor would a catalogue of all existing growth models prove that these inequalities are equals. But why try to square the circle? If we were unable to observe these inequalities, we would have to invent them because *they are the mainspring of economic growth.* They are the mainspring because they are the compelling economic force of growth. Thus, one of the essential parts of economic growth is concealed by such capital aggregation.

Another way of establishing the scope of this survey would be to extend the concept of human capital sufficiently to encompass all of the studies pertaining to manpower and to all aspects of human resources. I shall distinguish between these several concepts later in this section and indicate briefly the type of ambiguities that arise. Still another way of proceeding would be simply to list and then attempt to deal with the more important subfields that have emerged in this area. Such a list has the apparent advantage of appearing to be better suited for coping with real problems than a more generalized and abstract approach.

The list of subfields that follows is an indication of an array of studies that could be viewed either as falling within or as overlapping the boundaries of the domain of human capital: (1) manpower studies, (2) motivation and preferences of workers, (3) discrimination in the employment of workers of various ethnic groups, (4) unemployment by level of skills, age, sex, and by sectors, (5) migration within an economy by level of schooling, age, sex, and occupations, and among sectors, (6) migration between countries—the brain drain, (7) international trade implications of changes over time in the mix of labor skills, (8) differences in entrepreneurial abilities associated with different levels of educa-

[3] John Hicks, *Capital and Growth,* Oxford, Oxford University Press, 1965, Chapter 3, p. 35.

tion, (9) the supply of and demand for scientists and other highly skilled personnel, (10) the sources of poverty associated with lack of schooling, poor health, age, sex, and race, (11) the sources of the changes in the pattern of wages and salaries, (12) the factors that account for the tendency toward more equal distribution of personal income in the relatively rich, advanced countries, (13) the allocation of resources to and the efficiency with which they are used in economic activities that contribute to the formation of human capital—education, training of adults on the job, health, migration, and the search for information, (14) the economic connections between functional and personal distribution of income, closely related to (12) above, and (15) economic explanations and the economics of population growth. Long as this list may appear, let me repeat that it is by no means exhaustive.

From an analytical point of view, what is required is a classification of the various parts in accordance with economic theory. Because of the ambiguities that burden capital theory, we do well to bypass it, and rely on a theory of investment and the rates of return to investment opportunities.[4] Thus, the investment in human capital can conveniently be classified into investment in (1) schooling and higher education, (2) postschool training and learning, (3) preschool learning activities, (4) migration, (5) health, (6) information, and (7) investment in children (population). With respect to each of these investment activities, there are unsettled questions of economic efficiency and of equity. An integral part of this classification is the economic treatment of the allocation of time. In section III I shall rely in large part on this classification.

But we must go beyond this classification, meaningful as it may be in terms of activities, because it does not set the stage for an explicit reckoning of the supply of and demand for the new information that may be acquired by means of research. In section II below, the supply and demand considerations are introduced. There is both a short and a long horizon in developing new information that is valuable by virtue of the fact that it contributes to the advance in knowledge and is useful in making private and public decisions pertaining to human capital. I shall treat research as an *economic activity* because it uses scarce resources and because it produces new information that has an economic value. It must be said, however, that although the concept of human capital has become increasingly useful in economic analysis, all too little use has been made of it in clarifying policy choices. While most of the new

[4] The investment approach may also conceal particular underlying factors that require analysis.

studies in this area have policy implications, it is not always clear how the new information derived from them can serve those who are making the policy decisions that determine the allocation of resources to the many forms of human capital. Thus, even for the research results that are at hand, there is the task of decoding and interpreting this information with a view of making it meaningful in arriving at policy decisions.[5]

Before proceeding further, however, a comment is called for on the idea of human capital, the definition of the term "human capital," its roots in economics, and on the related concepts of "manpower" and "human resources." Human capital is strictly an economic concept. Although it pertains to particular attributes of man, it is not intended to serve those who are engaged in analyzing psychological, social, or cultural behavior. It is a form of capital because it is the source of future earnings, or of future satisfactions, or of both of them. It is *human* because it is an integral part of man. But human capital is not at home in the original house that economists built. The classical tripartite approach to the factors of production treats land as given by Nature, labor as workers who are capital-free, and capital as restricted to the material forms that are reproducible. Since improvements in land are man-made, they, too, may be treated as reproducible material capital, and consumer durables also qualify. The recent remodeling of growth economics tends toward two factor analyses, i.e., labor and capital, in which land may be added to the stock of capital at its capitalized value or omitted, presumably because of the small role that land plays in most modern economies. Nor is there a home for human capital in *Das Kapital* of Marx, for it, too, is restricted to the classical vintage of material capital. In short, the core of classical and neoclassical theories of production and distribution fails to take account of the capital component in labor. With respect to this failure, I have pointed out the following elsewhere: [6] "This notion of labor was wrong in the classical period and it is patently wrong now. Counting individuals who can and who want to work and treating such a count as a measure of the quality of an economic factor is no more meaningful than it would be to count the number of all manner of machines to determine their economic

[5] In my paper "The Human Capital Approach to Education," which appears as Chapter 2 in *Economic Factors Affecting the Financing of Education,* Roe L. Johns et al. (eds.), Gainesville, Fla., National Education Finance Project, 1970, I attempt to show the policy implications of the research results now available.

[6] Theodore W. Schultz, "Investment in Human Capital," *American Economic Review,* 51, March 1961, p. 3.

importance either as a stock of capital or as a flow of productive services. Laborers have become capitalists not from a diffusion of the ownership of corporation stocks, as folklore would have it, but from the acquisition of knowledge and skills that have economic value." [7]

What is required is an all-inclusive concept of capital that makes explicit the heterogeneity of capital in a dynamic economy adjusting to disequilibria as they are revealed by the inequalities in the rates of return. The core of such an all-inclusive concept of capital is not a recent invention. Irving Fisher clearly and cogently presented an all-inclusive concept of capital at the beginning of this century, starting with his paper "What Is Capital?" in 1896, elaborating on it in subsequent papers, and then completing the task in a classic book published in 1906.[8] Human capital is an integral part of Fisher's concept. (We are indebted to Kiker for his work on the historical roots of human capital.) [9]

But Fisher's approach to capital was not accepted by the mainstream of economists, mainly because of Marshall's adverse reactions to it, backed by his great prestige. Although Marshall at many points in his

[7] Two of my critics made the following extensions (quoted with permission from private correspondence):

Jacob Mincer: "It is a fascinating and paradoxical thought that the growth and spread of human capital accumulation by workers means that they have become capitalists even in 'communist' countries. At the same time, in 'capitalist' countries, this kind of capital accumulation is heavily subsidized and directed by the state. Thus, in the first set, the state is fostering the private ownership of such human means of production, while in the other set, the state is subsidizing the private ownership of human capital."

Samuel Bowles: ". . . The absence of any systematic treatment of human capital in either the classical or the Marxist scheme results from the fact that both Marx and the classical writers defined their factors of production in terms of the way they perceived the class structure of the period. The absence of any notion of human capital is . . . a result of a conscious attempt to portray the class structure as they saw it, coupled with the fact that the role of education and skills in the economy was considerably less than today. . . ."

[8] Irving Fisher, *The Nature of Capital and Income,* New York and London, Macmillan Company, 1906; also, "What Is Capital?," *Economic Journal,* 6, December 1896, pp. 509–34; "Senses of Capital," *Economic Journal,* 7, June 1897, pp. 199–213; and "Precedents for Defining Capital," *Quarterly Journal of Economics,* 18, March 1904, pp. 386–408.

[9] B. F. Kiker, "The Historical Roots of the Concept of Human Capital," *Journal of Political Economy,* 74, October 1966, pp. 481–99. Also, for a careful review of recent developments, see his *The Concept of Human Capital,* Essay in Economics No. 14, University of South Carolina, Bureau of Business and Economic Research, November 1966.

own work refers to the abilities man acquires by schooling and by working as an apprentice and to the economic role of knowledge, his view was
that, whereas human beings are incontestably capital from an abstract
and mathematical point of view, it would be impractical to extend the
traditional market place concept of capital to include human capital.
Ironically, the recent spate of rigorous mathematical economic growth
models, developed by economists who are not averse to using shadow
prices, have, with few exceptions,[10] also omitted human capital. They
treat labor as if it were capital-free. One of the reasons why these growth
models are lacking in explanatory power when applied empirically is the
omission of human capital, for it is this capital that has augmented the
quality of the labor force.

In using an all-inclusive concept of capital, it will be convenient as
a first approximation to think in terms of a dichotomy consisting of
human and nonhuman capital. It should be borne in mind as we proceed
that the forms of capital in both parts of this dichotomy are far from
homogeneous.[11] Furthermore, it is true that human capital has some
distinctive attributes. Whatever its form, it cannot be bought and sold
except where men are slaves.[12] Whereas material capital has the legal
status of property, human capital is not "protected" by this legal mantle,
slavery aside. For example, the freedom of choice in acquiring educational capital is subject to the difference in the legal status of human rights
and that of property. Since a person cannot indenture himself or enter
into a contract that would encumber his human rights, it follows that in the
case of a loan to a student for his education, the lender's property right in
the capital funds that he transfers to the student cannot be covered by a
mortgage on the student. When the appropriate job for a person, given
his education, is in another location, it is encumbent on him to migrate
to the new location to take advantage of his particular skills. If he is the
head of a household, the requirement would be that his entire family
would have to move to the new location. Married women are under

---

[10] One such exception is Assaf Razin's "Investment in Human Capital and
Economic Growth: A Theoretical Study," Ph.D. dissertation, University of
Chicago, 1969.

[11] They would be homogeneous for the analytical purpose at hand if, and
only if, each and every form of capital were rendering the same marginal rate of
return.

[12] The economic literature on the market value of slaves is substantial. For a
modern economic approach, see A. R. Conrad and J. R. Meyer, "The Economics of
Slavery in the Antebellum South," *Journal of Political Economy,* 66, April 1958,
pp. 95–130.

special social constraints in the use to which they can put their education in participating in the labor force because they are "tied" by marriage, which commits them, as a rule, to seeking a job appropriate to their skills in the particular location where their husbands work. *The most critical attribute of human capital arises from the fact that the person and his human capital are inseparable.* The person must always be personally present wherever the services of his human capital are being rendered.

While there are no markets in which human capital can be bought and sold, these forms of capital are nevertheless valuable to the person who possesses them because of the economic services they render. Most of the producer services of human capital carry price tags in terms of wages and salaries. For self-employed workers, it is the part of their income that is attributed to the work they do. The economic value of the services of the human capital that enters into entrepreneurial abilities is harder to come by.[13] But harder still is the task of determining the value of the consumer satisfactions that are derived from the stock of human capital that a person possesses. I am convinced, as I shall attempt to show in section III, that in national economic accounting it is now possible to evaluate and include the cost and returns associated with several important social goals that are presently not taken into account.

The economics of human capital as it has been developed during the last decade is, as already noted, of two general parts. The first emerges directly out of the theoretical core of economics in allocating investment resources in accordance with the priorities established by the relative rates of return on alternative investment opportunities, and then indirectly sets the stage for analyzing the particular economic effects of the formation and utilization of human capital upon the economic system, e.g., upon economic growth, upon the pattern of wages and salaries, and upon the distribution of personal income. The second part is the closely linked extension of earnings foregone in accordance with the development of the theory of time.

As a part of these introductory remarks, it should be noted that the concept of human capital is not synonymous with that of manpower or of human resources, although both of these are often used to cover a part of human capital. While I do not wish to imply that these concepts are not useful for some purposes, they are lacking in precision for the purpose at hand. Their limitations in this connection can be put quite simply.

[13] Finis Welch has broken new ground in this connection. See his "Education in Production," *Journal of Political Economy,* 78, No. 1, January/February 1970, pp. 35–59.

Whereas labor economics is being enriched by taking account of the human capital in the labor force, the measurement of manpower is still predominantly a head count of that part of the population that participates in the labor force, that is, laborers who want to work and who are employable. They are then classified in accordance with standard demographic characteristics, including, as a rule, their education. Although it is better than the classical concept of labor, it is nevertheless mainly an accounting of the number of laborers, even though it is adjusted for part-time employment and unemployment. Thus, it is not a strict economic accounting of the differences in the *quality* of the members of the labor force that plays an ever larger part in determining the effective labor input in a modern economy.

The term "human resources" is being used increasingly along with natural resources and other material resources. It is undoubtedly a useful descriptive term, but it is subject to ambiguities when it comes to economic analysis. Whereas natural resources and other material resources are passive economic factors in the sense that they are preference-free, *in the case of human agents it is necessary in undertaking an economic analysis to distinguish between their preferences and their abilities, including their skills and knowledge, as these abilities contribute to the possibilities of realizing their preferences.* Thus, my interpretation of the term "human resources" is that it encompasses all of the many attributes of a people—physical, biological, psychological, and cultural —that account for both the social values that determine preferences and the economic value of the producer and consumer services that a people render, whether they come to them as earnings or directly as personal satisfactions. The core of economic analysis rests on the assumption that preferences are given and that it is the function of economic activities to serve these preferences as best they can with the human and nonhuman capital at the disposal of the economy to obtain income streams and by transforming a part of this income by means of investment into additional forms of capital.

Since more than three-fourths of the income of a modern economy is attributed to the contributions of human agents, and hence a fourth or less to natural and other material forms of capital, it should be obvious that the formation and utilization of human capital is of major economic importance. The opening statement of my presidential address to the American Economic Association of a decade ago remains valid, i.e., ". . . that people acquire useful skills and knowledge . . . that these skills and knowledge are a form of capital, that this capital is in substantial part a product of deliberate investment, that it has grown in Western societies at a much faster rate than conventional (nonhuman) capital, and that its growth may well be the most distinctive feature of the economic system." [14]

I am acutely aware of a number of omissions in the material I cover in this paper. There is the method of analysis developed by Freeman to determine the responses to changes in demand by various classes of students in higher education and by faculty.[15] A part of the differences in motivations of students to perform in school can be explained by the differences in job opportunities; it is only touched on. Human capital in economic growth models is another omission, and the role of externalities still another. The testing of some hypotheses pertaining to human capital can be done better by appealing to historical data than by using short series of current data, in the manner of the studies by Fishlow and Solmon.[16] The neglect in empirical analysis of the satisfactions that accrue to students from the education they acquire is serious. It is an issue to which I have called attention repeatedly during recent years. There are several new hypotheses pertaining to fertility derived from economic theory that await testing.

Lastly, with regard to the scope of this paper, it is restricted to the U.S. economy and mainly to the work of U.S. economists on human capital. It is to this extent a parochial view. I regret this limitation, and all the more so in view of the many studies that have been made abroad predominantly in the area of schooling and higher education. The Canadian contributions parallel ours; in Western Europe, they tend to stress sociological considerations, or are strongly committed to programing models. In the United Kingdom, Professor Vaizey and associates continue to protest against the use of the earnings foregone concept, the applicability of rates of return analysis, and the omission of social considerations. Meanwhile, Professor Blaug and his colleagues have developed a strong research center.

I shall now turn to the factors that influence the costs of and returns to the new information acquired by means of research as the first step in developing a supply-demand approach in determining the research opportunities in the area of human capital.

[14] From the first paragraph of my "Investment in Human Capital," 1961, p. 1.

[15] Richard B. Freeman, *The Market for College-Trained Manpower: A Study in the Economics of Career Choice,* Cambridge, Harvard University Press, 1971.

[16] See Albert Fishlow, "Levels of Nineteenth Century American Investment in Education," *Journal of Economic History,* 26, December 1966, pp. 418–36, and Lewis C. Solmon, "Capital Formation by Expenditures on Formal Education, 1880 and 1890," Ph.D. dissertation, University of Chicago, 1968.

II. THE BUSINESS OF ECONOMIC RESEARCH

Research is an economic activity, the economics of which the economist neglects like the shoemaker the shoes of his children. Although economic research is a microscopic sector, it is not lacking in specialization. What is odd about this sector is that it is not organized to assemble the various specialized parts; instead, it is up to whoever uses them to determine where they belong in the economic system. Policymakers must do it themselves without an assembly kit. Under these conditions, who knows the research opportunities in human capital or in any of the other specialties? It is like asking who has a divining rod. It could be the policymakers, the congressional committees, the White House staff, and the public agencies that have a hand in administering public funds for education, health, and training for special jobs and the other public activities that affect the formation and utilization of human capital. Private foundations would claim this kind of competence, but for good reasons they are timid in proposing new research areas. Nonprofit organizations that specialize in economic research are presumably in the market for such a divining rod. Last on my list is the economist who is quick to submit a research proposal in response to the prospects of additional funds to support his enterprise.

Since studies in human capital fall into the domain of economics, it should be instructive to take a look at what economists do. Their professional behavior gives us several leads. What they do depends very much upon economic theory, quantitative techniques, and data possibilities for undertaking empirical work. They occasionally come upon unresolved economic puzzles that challenge their curiosity. Some of them respond to the demands of private and public agents for economic information. They are subject to the constraints of the resources at their disposal in augmenting the supply of economic information by means of organized research. These are the things that make economists tick and they are highly complementary.

As I pursue these leads, I shall define economic research as a specialized activity that requires special skills and facilities that are employed to discover and develop new economic information. By this definition it is an *economic activity* that requires scarce resources and that produces something of value. The scarce resources that are allocated to this research are readily observed and measured. But the value it renders is exceedingly hard to get at. It renders satisfactions to research workers, in part because it is a way of acquiring professional recognition and in part because of the personal value that researchers place on it for its own sake. There are also some social satisfactions, even national prestige, in winning the recently established Nobel Prize in economics. But more important is the value that the new economic information derives from the demand for it by households, firms, and agencies of government. In general, then, the value of this research is of two basic parts: (1) the value of satisfactions that accrue to research workers and to society; and (2) the value that this new information renders in terms of services to those who utilize it in their activities.[17] Since such new information is valuable, it is permissible and appropriate to look upon the allocation of resources to support research as an investment.

In evaluating human capital research, there are five supply-demand considerations, each of which I shall consider briefly:

1. Changes that have been occurring in the state of economics.
2. The role that economic puzzles play in what economists do in their research.
3. A brief reference to the amount of resources and the restrictions imposed on them.
4. The response of economists to the demand for their product.
5. Some additional reflections on the attributes of the demand.

1. Changes in Economics

Research in economics has flourished during recent decades. Its growth is explained in large part by the advances in economic theory and quantitative techniques, and in the adequacy and reliability of data. In short, as in other sectors, the production possibilities in economics have improved. If economists were to measure their own productivity as they have that of the economy they would also discover a large residual!

At the risk of seeming presumptuous, I shall venture a comment on what has been happening to the analytical equipment in economics and the prowess of economists in using it. My foil will be the perceptive appraisal of my colleague, Harry G. Johnson.[18] Economic theory has been

[17] For an extended treatment of this approach, see my *Investment in Human Capital: The Role of Education and of Research,* New York, Free Press, 1971, Chapter 12.

[18] Harry G. Johnson's "The Economic Approach to Social Questions," his inaugural lecture delivered at The London School of Economics and Political Science, October 12, 1967, was published in *Economica,* 36, February 1968, pp. 1–21. The thrust of Mary Jean Bowman's "The Human Investment Revolution in Economic Thought" is also very relevant to the task at hand. It appears in *Sociology of Education,* 39, Spring 1966, pp. 111–37.

extended and made more rigorous; the advances in quantitative techniques have been even more pronounced; and improvements in data supplied mainly by federal agencies have contributed much to the advances in empirical analysis. Empirical testing of economic hypotheses has prospered, especially so in this country. We owe much to macro economics. Meanwhile, micro economics has been enlarged and strengthened by a number of new developments. In general, economics has become more robust and the economist more sophisticated in the treatment of values and in the analysis of major social questions, in considerable part as a consequence of the extension of theory based on human capital.

Professor Johnson, in my view, is correct in arguing that economic theorizing, research, and public discussion have overplayed macro economics in concentrating on income and employment, economic growth models, and increasing the rate of growth "to the neglect of micro-economic problems of efficient resource allocation whose solutions are likely to be over the long run more important to the achievement of a highly productive and rapidly growing economy." [19] The intellectual achievement of Keynes in coping with the problem of unemployment laid the foundations of macro economics. When that problem is solved and we attain a fully employed economy, the main concern of economic analysis "is with the micro-economic problems of allocating scarce resources among competing uses, these uses being defined to include provision for the satisfaction of future needs." [20] The empirical work of analyzing these micro-economic problems is also dependent on aggregation and thus it, too, has benefited from the advances in quantitative techniques in treating aggregates.

Professor Johnson presents six recent developments in economics that have significant implications for broader social questions. Two of them pertain to fundamental economic principles and the treatment of values in economic analysis, and four to new approaches. Since his presentation leads directly into the role of human capital, I shall quote him at some length at this point. [21]

> The "robustness" of a theory means the extent to which its conclusions survive under changes in the assumptions from which it is derived. In the 1930s, in the heyday of the imperfect-monopolistic competition revolution, it came to be widely believed that the conclusions of neo-classical economic analysis were crucially de-

[19] Ibid., p. 2.
[20] Ibid., p. 3.
[21] Ibid., pp. 5–10.

pendent on a long list of "unrealistic" abstractions, such as perfect
knowledge, perfect competition, and rational utility or profit max-
imization on the part of economic decisions-takers. . . . The
subsequent rise of "positive" economics has shifted the emphasis
from testing the reality or plausibility of the assumptions to testing
the robustness of the conclusions of a theory, a test which may be
conducted either by empirical estimation or by theoretical investigation; and the results have almost invariably been to confirm and
strengthen the main propositions of abstract theory. Thus it has
been shown, for example, that imperfect competition theory yields
virtually no testable positive predictions that might be inconsistent
with the theory of pure competition; that whether firms consciously
seek to maximize profits and minimize costs or not, competition will
eliminate the inefficient firms; and that whether consumer behaviour
is rational or purely random, the demand curves for products will
tend to slope downwards as in the Marshallian analysis.

With regard to the treatment of values and value judgments in
economics, the neo-classical tradition . . . carried a strong presumption in favour of *laissez-faire* as the policy required to maximize economic welfare. That presumption was destroyed by Lionel
Robbins' *The Nature and Significance of Economic Science,* which
denied the very possibility of handling value judgments scientifically.
The "new welfare economics," which emerged rapidly in response to
Robbins' challenge, has made economists much more aware of the
pervasiveness and relevance of value judgments in economic analysis
and prescription, and much more careful about treating them explicitly.

Three of the four new approaches that Professor Johnson identifies
are integral parts of the developments in human capital. The fourth pertains to public policy in a democracy. I shall introduce the three pertaining to human capital here, and shall examine some of their implications
for research later in this survey.

The first of these . . . [pertains] . . . to the economics of
the role of human beings in the productive process—based on the
concept of "human capital." According to this concept, the skilled
(or even the so-called "unskilled") worker, and the academically
or professionally trained executive, are envisaged as particular
types of capital equipment employed in the production process, in
the sense that their capacity to make a contribution to the produc-

tive process is developed by a process of investment (which means simply the sacrifice of current resources for future returns) incurred in the formal education system and through on-the-job training, and that this investment yields its returns over the life-time of the individual concerned. It should be noted that the concept of investment in the formation of human capital extends readily beyond the education system, into the economics of such apparently unrelated phenomena as immigration and emigration and the social value of medical care. . . . The concept of human capital has tremendous integrative power, in that it provides a unifying principle for the consistent explanation of many phenomena of the labour market. Perhaps its most fundamental implication, from the point of view of social thought, is that the worker in an advanced industrial economy is typically a very considerable capitalist. . . . A second implication, which is extremely relevant to the broad question of social and economic inequality, is that the economic rewards for alternative occupations and careers need to be compared in terms of life-time income profiles, and not in terms of the highest annual income earned in the course of the career. . . . A third implication, also relevant to the question of inequality, is that in their choices among alternative possible careers, new entrants to the labour force face the same problems of assembling information, assessing risks, evaluating returns, and obtaining the resources for investment, as do prospective investors in material capital equipment or in stocks and shares.

The second important new development in economic analysis is the treatment of time as the fundamental unit of cost in individual allocative decisions with respect to both labour and consumption. This conception is to be distinguished sharply from the classical treatment of labour-time used up in production as the determinant of economic value; and its usefulness derives from the characteristics of the affluent modern economy, in which the typical consumer has a standard of living stratospherically above mere subsistence and is constantly required to choose among competing consumer goods. The central principle of the analysis is that in reality each consumer good has two prices attached to it—a money price, as in the traditional theory of consumer choice, and a time cost of acquiring and consuming the commodity.

The third important new development in economics is the recognition that the information required for the making of choices is not a free good, but has a cost of acquisition that may not be worth paying. In view of the cost of acquiring the requisite information, relative to its value in improving the outcome of the decision-making process, it is natural to expect that many decisions, even some quite important ones, will be taken on the basis of extremely fragmentary information, or by rules of thumb, or on the basis of information provided in persuasive capsule form by parties interested in influencing the outcome of decisions.[22]

To summarize, the "robustness" of the pure theory of competition has been reaffirmed as the analytical limitations of imperfect-monopolistic competition have become clear. The treatment of values and value judgments by economists no longer rests on a monolithic presumption in favor of *laissez-faire* in the choice of policy to maximize economic welfare. The importance of macro economics in solving the problem of unemployment is firmly established, but the economic growth models are not solving the problem of economic development. In allocating scarce resources efficiently in such economies, the allocative problems once again call for micro-economic analysis. Meanwhile, the advances in economic theory and quantitative techniques and the increasing availability of data have greatly extended the analytical capacity of micro economics. But for all that, economic analysis has contributed little to the solutions of the problems associated with the inequalities in the distribution of personal income and wealth.

2. Role of Economic Puzzles

Puzzles provide clues to what economists do. But more important for the purpose at hand, they are a guide to some of the better research

[22] Professor Johnson cites several references in connection with this material, including: Milton Friedman, "The Methodology of Positive Economics," in his *Essays in Positive Economics,* Chicago, 1953, pp. 3–43; George C. Archibald, "Chamberlin Versus Chicago," in *Review of Economic Studies,* 29, October 1961, pp. 1–28; Armen Alchian, "Uncertainty, Evolution, and Economic Theory," in *Journal of Political Economy,* 58, June 1950, pp. 211–21; Gary S. Becker, "Irrational Behavior and Economic Theory," in *Journal of Political Economy,* 70, February 1962, pp. 1–13, as well as his *Human Capital: A Theoretical and Empirical Analysis, with Special Reference to Education,* New York, NBER, 1964, and "A Theory of the Allocation of Time," in *Economic Journal,* 75, September 1965, pp. 493–517; Theodore W. Schultz (ed.), "Investment in Human Beings," *Journal of Political Economy,* 70, October 1962 supplement; and George J. Stigler, "The Economics of Information," *Journal of Political Economy,* 69, June 1961, pp. 213–25.

opportunities. It is conventional to refer to theoretical issues and their implications that are in doubt as unsettled economic questions, and to refer to casual observations of economic behavior that appear to be incompatible with received theory as paradoxes, e.g., the Giffen Paradox. As more and better data have become available and as empirical work has come into its own, the measurement of economic relationships and the testing of hypotheses frequently reveal behavior and developments that are inconsistent one with another or with received theory. These inconsistencies are here viewed as puzzles. They are especially challenging, as is evident from the professional papers that begin with a puzzle which the author then attempts to resolve.

The advances in the measurement of income, in substantial part the result of research sponsored by the National Bureau of Economic Research, and the particular estimates of capital and labor as inputs that followed set the stage for Abramovitz's paper announcing *The Residual*.[23] There it was, yet by all the canons of economics it could not be accepted, except as a measure of our ignorance. Why was the rate of output increase so much higher than that of the inputs? What had been ignored? No wonder then that this residual became the takeoff for much research to discover the sources of the unexplained increases in output. Closely akin is the puzzle pertaining to the increases in U.S. agricultural output that were occurring in spite of the fact that there were virtually no increases in measured agricultural inputs—the puzzle that challenged Griliches.[24] Another important puzzle stemmed from the inconsistency in the results from time series data and from cross-sectional data pertaining to the proportion of the personal income that people save as their income increases.[25]

The research opportunities in the area of human capital are in no small measure revealed by various economic puzzles. With regard to the

[23] Moses Abramovitz, *Resources and Output Trends in the United States Since 1870*, NBER, Occasional Paper No. 52, 1956.

[24] Zvi Griliches, "The Sources of Measured Productivity Growth: United States Agriculture, 1940–1960," *Journal of Political Economy*, 71, August 1963, pp. 331–46; and "Research Expenditures, Education, and the Aggregate Agricultural Production Function," *American Economic Review*, 54, December 1964, pp. 961–74. For an earlier awareness of this puzzle and how it might be solved, see my *The Economic Organization of Agriculture*, New York, McGraw-Hill, 1953, Chapter 7; and then, with more insight, my "Reflections on Agricultural Production, Output, and Supply," *Journal of Farm Economics*, 38, August 1958, pp. 748–62.

[25] Milton Friedman, *A Theory of the Consumption Function*, Princeton, Princeton University Press for NBER, 1957.

first set of puzzles referred to above, it is now established that the omission of the improvements in the labor force associated with education accounted for a large underestimation of the increases in the effective labor force, as Denison as well as Jorgenson and Griliches have shown.[26] For U.S. agriculture, the schooling of the labor force has about the same weight as the head count of labor in what each contributes to agricultural production.[27]

The residual, however, is only one of many economic puzzles that have emerged mainly from recent empirical work. While they reflect the growing pains of economics, they are also challenging research opportunities. It is in this sense that I think of them as influencing the supply of new information that is acquired by means of research. At this point, it will suffice to list some of these puzzles and then later on elaborate on these and on other puzzles.

The four that follow are by no means a complete listing of such puzzles. They may, however, serve as a preliminary step in taking our bearings. (1) Kuznets's estimates show that the pace of capital formation in the United States has been slowing down; [28] it means that net capital formation has been declining relative to the increases in national income. The implications of these estimates are beset by puzzles with respect to savings and to the role of capital in a country that is deemed to be ever more highly capital-intensive. (2) Although the United States is a capital-rich country and, in accordance with the theory of comparative advantage, our exports should consist predominantly of capital-intensive products, they are in fact in large part labor-intensive—an inconsistency that is known as the Leontief Paradox. (3) Next on this preliminary list are the large increases in the real earnings of workers. Surely these additional earnings are no mere windfalls; nor are they quasi rents pending the adjustment of the labor supply, nor are they a pure rent on the inherited abilities of workers.[29] (4) The distribution of personal *income*

[26] Edward F. Denison, *The Sources of Economic Growth in the United States and the Alternatives Before Us,* New York, Committee for Economic Development, 1962; also, my "Education and Economic Growth" in *Social Forces Influencing American Education,* Nelson B. Henry, ed., Chicago, University of Chicago Press, 1961; and D. W. Jorgenson and Zvi Griliches, "The Explanation of Productivity Change," *Review of Economic Studies,* 34, July 1967, pp. 249–83.

[27] See papers by Griliches cited above.

[28] Simon Kuznets, assisted by Elizabeth Jenks, *Capital in the American Economy: Its Formation and Financing,* Princeton, Princeton University Press for NBER, 1961.

[29] Barry R. Chiswick, "Earnings Inequality and Economic Development," *Quarterly Journal of Economics,* 85, February 1971, pp. 21–39.

has become more equal since the beginning of this century in those Western European countries for which there are adequate income data to measure this development as well as in the United States,[30] although estimates of the distribution of personal *wealth* in the case of the United States show that it has not only remained very unequal but has changed very little over time.[31] Prima facie these two sets of estimates appear to be inconsistent.

The resolution of these four basic puzzles, as in the case of the residual, is dependent in large part on human capital.

3. Resources for Economic Research

Economic research has been enjoying a growth rate that puts the growth of GNP to shame. There are now all manner of economic research enterprises and many of them have "just growed" like Topsy. Only a few of them have been around long enough to become as mature in their behavior as the National Bureau.

The amount of resources and the conditions imposed on their use obviously influence the supply that is here under consideration. To keep this paper within reasonable bounds, I shall not enter upon an examination of the availability of such resources. In the discussion that follows I touch on some of the weaknesses of the organization of economic research.

4. Response to Demand

Economic research is no longer merely a simple cottage industry as it once was on our campuses when university-employed economists now and then found some time to do research, provided they were willing to neglect their regular university duties. As economics has prospered, how-

[30] Simon Kuznets, "Economic Growth and Income Inequality," *American Economic Review,* 45, March 1955, pp. 1–28; "Quantitative Aspects of Economic Growth of Nations: Part VIII, Distribution of Income by Size," *Economic Development and Cultural Change,* II, No. 2, Part II, January 1963; and *Modern Economic Growth,* New Haven, Yale University Press, 1966; T. Paul Schultz, "The Distribution of Income: Case Study of the Netherlands," Ph.D. dissertation, Massachusetts Institute of Technology, 1965; and "Secular Trends and Cyclical Behavior of Income Distribution in the United States: 1944–1965," in *Six Papers on the Size Distribution of Wealth and Income,* Lee Soltow, ed., New York, NBER, 1969.

[31] Robert J. Lampman, *The Share of Top Wealth-Holders in National Wealth, 1922–1956,* Princeton, Princeton University Press for NBER, 1962.

ever, research has become increasingly an organized activity consisting of many different types of enterprises. University duties have been redefined not only to provide time for research but, more than that, to give it a high priority as a university activity. Meanwhile, many governmental agencies have established economic research units mainly to undertake program analyses appropriate to their area of activity. Large business corporations have evolved a similar pattern in establishing economic research units to serve them in making program decisions. Another important development, especially so in this country, has been the private not-for-profit research organization. Thus, economic research activities have proliferated, for there has been rapid growth and an increasing division of labor and specialization. But for all that no economist to my knowledge has investigated the efficiency of these economic research enterprises, or, more specifically for the purpose at hand, of their responses to changes in the demand for economic information. Would that we had such a study. Although a few reflections on my part on this issue are a poor substitute for the analysis that is lacking, it must suffice.

My own view is, then, that the lags in these responses on the part of economists are in general not long and of secondary importance compared to the adverse effects on research of the mistakes in identifying the demand for new economic information. The demand is poorly identified for the following reasons:

1. Program demands are served and policy is neglected. Although the literature in economics is strongly oriented toward policy issues, the use of the term "policy" is as a rule superficial because it fails to take account of the interdependence of the many parts of the political and economic system. In turn, most economic research is in response to the demand of specific programs, in spite of the fact that what may be good for a particular program is bad for the economy.[32]

2. The specialization in economic research is not well attuned to changes in demand with a view to distinguishing between what is and what is not important. The advantages of specialization in economic research are often offset by substantial losses that arise from the chronic lack of integration between its several parts. While I would like to believe that university research enterprises are immune to losses of this nature, experience tells me this is not true. The process of achieving integration may be stronger in economics departments that in fact operate as departments and not as a loose conglomeration of fiefdoms than within

[32] For a perceptive paper on this issue, see Daniel P. Moynihan, "The Concept of Public Policy in the 1970s," delivered at Hendrix College, April 6, 1970, unpublished, The White House, Washington, D.C.

other types of research organizations. The problem here is, of course, closely akin to that of (1) above, and the required solution is the same. The core of economic theory is indispensable in recognizing, specifying, and analyzing the interdependency of the parts of the economic system.

3. There is a strong tendency to conceive of these demands as a call for more statistics and more econometric models, with all too little attention to the economics of problems that are inherent in such demands for new information.

4. In assessing the formulation of these demands, specialized research organizations find it exceedingly difficult to acquire the criticism of competent outside economists who are not "tied" by the sources of their own research funds and who are not all too specialized in the particular area of research.

Thus far, I have been concerned predominantly with the responses to the demands of public agencies, and I have argued that the lags in the response of economists are of minor importance compared to short-comings in the way these demands are formulated and approached in economic research. I would be remiss, however, if I did not call attention to the general neglect of the private demands for economic information. In the area of human capital, it is the private demand for information by households that has not been served. Responses by economists to it are virtually nil, largely because of the fragmented market, which fails to reveal this demand adequately.

5. Further Reflections on the Demand

Although the price of economists has become high, the per unit cost of producing new economic information has undoubtedly been declining as a consequence of the advances in analytical equipment. It would be simple if the additional demand could be explained by Say's Law. Nor would it be difficult to merely list the many public programs, each with its particular demand. But neither of these two approaches would be very fruitful.

The demand of firms for their own research output is readily determined from the point of view of economic analysis under the assumptions that they operate for profit, that their research is confined to producing results that they can appropriate, and that they are informed about the research possibilities and the potential economic value of the results. Casual observation of their behavior suggests that it is the last of these three assumptions that may be in doubt. But some of the more valuable parts of the new information won by research consist of new ideas, advances in economic theory and in quantitative techniques that are not appropriable. They are not sufficiently specific to be patented. Since it is not possible to "control" their utilization, they are normally published in economic journals and monographs, and when this has occurred they are in the public domain and thus accessible to anyone. The results of most empirical research, including that which is undertaken to serve public programs or to serve persons in making private decisions, are also, as a rule, placed in the public domain. Most economic research is not undertaken by firms *for profit;* the primary part is financed and administered by agencies that operate *not for profit*. These agencies, accordingly, are the main suppliers here under consideration.

A summary of the supply and demand considerations that influence economic research must begin with the dynamics of our research activities. These dynamic attributes are especially acute in the recent extensions of economics into the area of human capital. They reveal many new, unexhausted research opportunities. The primary development is a consequence of the advances in economic theory, in quantitative techniques, and in tools and data that make possible highly sophisticated empirical analyses. Recent empirical work reveals a number of economic puzzles that account for some of the fruitful research in the recent past and also provide important clues for future research. With respect to the response of economists to the demands for their product, the lags in this response are not unduly long, so it seems to me. *These demands are, however, poorly identified: particular public program demands are overemphasized and, as a consequence, policy demands that take account of the interdependency of the critical parts of the economic and political system and the demand of the private human capital sector are neglected.* Much of the research here under consideration emerges from the allocation of funds administered by agencies that operate not for profit. The performance of these agencies is not subject to strong economic incentives. The role of foundations in this connection is far from settled. In allocating their funds, they serve mainly the curiosity of their staffs and trustees. But to the extent that they are program-oriented to the neglect of policy-oriented economic research, the curiosity that is supported is less than optimum in terms of social benefits.

III. AN OFFERING OF RESEARCH OPPORTUNITIES

I am ready to start the auction. Since it is early and the light is still dim, let me assure you that there are no antiques among the research projects that are up for sale. They are mostly new ideas that have not been tested and there is no guarantee that they will pan out. Since research is shrouded in uncertainty, it will suffice to deal in shadow prices provided it is understood that the invisible hand of supply and demand is shaping the course of this auction.

My plan is to begin with research opportunities that are dimly revealed in public and private "demands" for new economic information pertaining to the formation and utilization of human capital. Next, I intend to return to some of the research implications of particular economic puzzles. Lastly, I shall consider what is undoubtedly the most important development affecting the supply of research opportunities, namely, the advances in economic theory and in recent empirical work.

PUBLIC AND PRIVATE DEMANDS BY CLASSES OF POLICY ISSUES

It would be in good grace as well as convenient to offer research projects that would strengthen the case for more investment in human capital. But the problems that await solution cannot be treated in so convenient a manner. From the point of view of economic analysis, there are two fundamental problems in economic policy choices, namely, *efficiency* and *equity*. The test of economic efficiency of a particular public program in terms of its own particular purpose I shall call "specific efficiency." When the economic test is extended to take account of all of the effects that a program has on the economic system, I shall call it the "general efficiency" test. The other basic problem in policy choices that awaits clarification and solution pertains to the effects of programs upon equity, i.e., upon the distribution of personal income.

In serving the private demand for information in this area, the problem is solely one of allocative efficiency on private account, unless the economic inequities within the family are raised. It is difficult, however, to identify the private demand; it is even less visible than the public demand. It is, nevertheless, pervasive and exceedingly important in improving private allocative decisions with an eye to economic efficiency.

Despite the progress in dealing with social questions, it still is true that the hallmark of economic analysis is economic efficiency. It stands for rigorous analytical workmanship when it is not encumbered by the problem of equity, i.e., the distribution of personal income. But it is seldom that the realization of additional economic efficiency is neutral in its effects upon the distribution of personal income. As yet, the tradeoff choices between efficiency and equity are not clearly established, and when they become known the choice that matters depends on the values that determine social preferences. What is often overlooked, however, is the fact that there are policy choices where additional economic efficiency will also contribute to the social goal of reducing the inequality in the distribution of personal income. This is frequently true in the area of human capital.[33]

The discussion that follows will be in eight parts: (1) schooling and higher education: the question of equity; (2) schooling and higher education: economic efficiency; (3) postschool investment in human capital; (4) preschool investment in human capital; (5) human capital approach to migration; (6) health as an investment; (7) the search for information; and (8) the acquisition of children. Note that the treatment of schooling and higher education will be in two parts, one dealing with the question of equity and the other with allocative efficiency. Since schooling and higher education encompass the most important set of programs contributing to the formation of human capital and since the work by economists in this area is the most advanced in providing fairly firm benchmarks, my survey of it will be much more extensive than that of the others.

1. Schooling and Higher Education: The Question of Equity

This question should be high on our research list. What are the effects of schooling and higher education upon the distribution of personal income? In view of the ways in which education is financed and the benefits of education are distributed among the population—are the net results progressive, neutral, or regressive? However efficient the educational enterprise may become in the allocation of funds to its many parts and in the uses that are made of them, the problem of equity will be with us. Because of the magnitude of our educational activities, it is understandable that it should be a major social question. National concern about this problem is bound to increase, especially so in congressional committees and in public discussions pertaining to the allocation of federal funds to education.

If these equity effects were neutral, or if they were progressive and thus in line with widely held social values, the problem would not be on my research agenda. But there are growing doubts about what, in fact, these equity effects are in our society. The presumption is strong, and

[33] W. Lee Hansen makes the point that since the domain where equity and efficiency policy choices converge is probably large, it should receive special attention.

it is being supported by some empirical work, that all is not well in higher education on this score. In making the case for vast increases in public and private funds for higher education, it will not suffice simply to stress the cultural satisfactions and producer services that accrue to students privately and to society in terms of social externalities. Nor is it sufficient to argue for "equal opportunity" in higher education: it could simply mean subsidizing all qualified students and leaving the equity question unresolved.

In taking one's bearings on the equity problem, there are three propositions with implications that provide some guidance. (1) Since the distribution of personal income from nonhuman capital (income-producing property) is much more unequal than that from human capital, and as the stock of human capital increases relative to that of nonhuman capital, other things being equal, the inequality in the distribution of personal income is thereby reduced.[34] (2) To the extent that the number of years and the quality of schooling, both elementary and high school, the children of all families acquire approach equality, and to the extent that the differences in innate ability account for a small part of economic value of such schooling, the inequality in the personal distribution of earnings (income) is thereby reduced. (3) Although there are appreciable rents to innate abilities that are necessary to acquire the skills and knowledge associated with higher education,[35] if all students (their families) were to pay the full cost of the education they receive, the unequal distribution of innate abilities per se would not increase the inequality in distribution of personal income that originates from higher education.

In clarifying further the implications of the first of these propositions, it may be helpful to introduce several highly simplifying assumptions along with the following concepts. Let me begin with raw labor and define it as encompassing no human capital (a concept of convenience for the purpose at hand). Raw labor consists of "bodies" with a capability that can be thought of as brute force. Although females and children have less of this component than adult males, let us assume that each household (family) has the same mix and amount of raw labor at its disposal. Under the assumption that the earnings of this raw labor were the same for every household in the economy, the distribution of

---

[34] This proposition is advanced as a hypothesis in my "Reflections on Investment in Man," *Journal of Political Economy*, 70, October 1962, supplement, p. 2.

[35] See my hypothesis of this under point 6 on pp. 69–70 below.

personal income among households from this source would be equal. We now consider nonhuman capital, income-producing property, and assume that the ownership of such capital is highly concentrated—say, all of it belongs to ten per cent of the households. Assume, further, that the accumulation of additional nonhuman capital takes place at a higher rate than the rate of increase of households (raw labor) and that the rate of return to the capital stays constant. It follows that the distribution of personal income between the ninety per cent of households that have only raw labor and the ten per cent that own all of the nonhuman capital would become more unequal.[36] We now introduce human capital and assume that it is acquired by all households and that it is distributed equally among households. Assume, also, that the rate of return to such human capital is somewhat higher than that derived from nonhuman capital and that the accumulation of additional human capital takes place at a higher rate than the rate of increase in nonhuman capital, induced by the difference in the rates of return. As the accumulation of human capital occurs at a higher rate than the rate of increase in households (raw labor), it follows that this process would tend to reduce the inequality in the distribution of personal income between the ninety per cent of households with none of the nonhuman capital and the ten per cent that own all of the income-producing property.[37]

There are strong reasons for distinguishing between schooling and higher education in attacking this problem. The attributes that account for this distinction lead me to propose the following two hypotheses:

One: *Elementary schools and high schools in the United States are in general somewhat progressive in their effects on the distribution of personal income.*

Two: *Higher education in the United States, leaving community colleges aside, is substantially regressive in its effects upon the distribution of personal income.*

In undertaking well-conceived research on this problem of equity, the analytical cupboard is not bare, in no small part due to contributions from work sponsored by the National Bureau of Economic Research.

[36] Unequal is defined in terms of relative means of the two groups and also in terms of their absolute difference.

[37] A workshop held at the University of Chicago, June 7–10, 1971, in which twenty economists participated with eight major papers under consideration, dealt with various aspects of the effects of higher education on the distribution of personal income. These papers and comments are to appear as a supplement to the *Journal of Political Economy* in May/June, 1972.

Becker's approach in his *Human Capital and the Personal Distribution of Income* is basic.[38] Preceding Becker, there is the pioneer work of Mincer in his Ph.D. research and his 1958 paper, and his excellent recent survey of the analytical developments in this area, including further major contributions of his own.[39] Mincer's survey gives us an up-to-date analytical framework for undertaking research concerned with the distribution of earnings, leaving the income from property aside.[40] In addition, there are the empirical results from Chiswick; the analysis by Hansen and Weisbrod of public higher education in California (concluding that the net results are regressive in their effects on the distribution of personal income); three comments on an abridged version of the Hansen-Weisbrod findings, and a disagreement with their conclusions by Pechman, the final section of whose paper dealing with the "Implications of Distributional Data" adds strong support to my view that research on this important equity problem should be given a high priority.[41]

[38] Gary S. Becker, *Human Capital and the Personal Distribution of Income: An Analytical Approach*, Woytinsky Lecture No. 1, Institute of Public Administration and Department of Economics, University of Michigan, Ann Arbor, Michigan, 1967.

[39] Jacob Mincer, "A Study of Personal Income Distribution," Ph.D. dissertation, Columbia University, 1957; "Investment in Human Capital and Personal Income Distribution," *Journal of Political Economy*, 66, August 1958, pp. 281–302; and "The Distribution of Labor Incomes: A Survey with Special Reference to the Human Capital Approach," *Journal of Economic Literature*, 8, March 1970, pp. 1–26.

[40] For substantial advances in economic thinking on the equity and efficiency issues with special reference to higher education, see the supplement referred to in footnote 37.

[41] For relevant studies, see Barry R. Chiswick, "Human Capital and the Personal Income Distribution by Regions," Ph.D. dissertation, Columbia University, 1967; W. Lee Hansen and Burton A. Weisbrod, *Benefits, Costs, and Finance of Public Higher Education*, Chicago, Markham, 1969, and "The Distribution of Costs and Direct Benefits of Public Higher Education: The Case of California," *Journal of Human Resources*, 4, Spring 1969, pp. 176–91; three comments on the latter paper by Hansen and Weisbrod by Elchanan Cohn, Adam Gifford, and Ira Sharkansky in the *Journal of Human Resources*, 5, Spring 1970, pp. 222–36; and Joseph A. Pechman, "The Distributional Effects of Public Higher Education in California," *Journal of Human Resources*, 5, Summer 1970, pp. 361–70.

The analytical cupboard also contains the following studies:

Gary S. Becker and Barry R. Chiswick, "Education and the Distribution of Earnings," *American Economic Review*, 56, May 1966, pp. 358–69; Barry R. Chiswick, "The Average Level of Schooling and the Personal Distribution of Income by Regions: A Clarification," *American Economic Review*, 58, June 1968, pp. 495–500; Thomas Johnson, "Returns from Investment in Schooling and On-the-Job Training," Ph.D. dissertation, North Carolina State University, 1969, and

2. Schooling and Higher Education: Economic Efficiency

It is fair to say that we do not have an economic policy that encompasses education; nor do we have even a partial economic policy to optimize the many different classes of educational expenditures. Although the total annual expenditure on regular schooling and higher education in the United States now exceeds $70 billion,[42] an accounting which does not include the earnings foregone by students nor the expenditures on programs complementary to education, there is no policy to integrate in terms of cost and benefits these educational expenditures among schools and among programs to which funds are allocated, despite the magnitude of the expenditures and the heterogeneity of the educational enterprises. Even if every public program were efficient in terms of its specific purpose, it would be astonishing if we were to discover that each and every educational program met the test of general economic efficiency. On the contrary, we would expect and we are beginning to identify some of the malallocations within the educational complex. But the task of investigating the sources and the extent of the lack of general economic efficiency in this area presents a large set of research opportunities that will continue to go by the board if they are left to the research units of the major school systems, state educational bodies, and the many ongoing federal programs.

Whether the allocation of resources to education is in the public or private domain, the central economic concept in planning and financing education, abstracting from equity considerations, is the rate of return on the educational investments, and the general efficiency test is that this investment be made in accordance with the priorities set by the relative rates of return on alternative investment opportunities. This concept has a firm foundation in economic theory, it is applicable both to public and private investment decisions, and it is widely used and understood in practical affairs.

his "Returns from Investment in Human Capital," *American Economic Review*, 60, September 1970, pp. 546–60; Jacob Mincer, "Schooling, Age, and Earnings," NBER, preliminary typescript, 1969; Lee Soltow (ed.), *Six Papers on the Size Distribution of Wealth and Income*, Columbia University Press for NBER, 1969; T. Paul Schultz, "The Distribution of Income: Case Study of The Netherlands," 1965, and his *Personal Income Distribution Statistics of the United States*, prepared for the Joint Economic Committee of Congress, 1965.

[42] The National Education Association, in *Financial Status of Public Schools, 1970*, Washington, D.C., 1970, p. 31, places the 1969–70 public expenditures at $54.1 billion and the private expenditures at $12.7 billion, and shows the recent rate of increase at 8.8 per cent.

TABLE 1

Estimates of Private Rates of Returns, United States
(*per cent*)

Year	High School Graduates (White Males, After Personal Taxes) [a]	College Graduates (White Males, After Personal Taxes) [a]	Corporate Manufacturing Firms (After Profit Taxes but Before Personal Taxes) [b]	U.S. Private Domestic Economy (Implicit Rate of Returns After Profit Taxes but Before Personal Taxes) [c]
1939	16	14.5		—
1949	20	13.+		12.6
1956	25	12.4	7.0 (for period	14.4 (1955–56)
1958	28	14.8	1947–57)	12.3 (1957–58)
1959	Slightly higher than in 1958			9.7
1961	Slightly higher than in 1958			11.2 (1960–61)
1963–65	—	—		13.3

Source: Theodore W. Schultz, "Resources for Higher Education: An Economist's View," *Journal of Political Economy,* May/June 1968, p. 337.

[a] From Gary S. Becker, *Human Capital,* 1964, p. 128.

[b] Ibid., p. 115 and n. 2, where Becker draws on a study by George J. Stigler.

[c] Jorgenson and Griliches, "The Explanation of Productivity Change," p. 268.

Rate of Returns Indications.   Before I turn to the inferences supported by the recent research results that imply that there are substantial malallocations among the educational enterprises, it will be necessary to review briefly the rate of returns profile that characterizes U.S. education on the basis of the research results already at hand.[43] For higher education, these results indicate that the rate of returns is, in general, in line with the rate of returns in the economy as a whole. High school ranks high by this test, and elementary schooling is at the top in a ranking by rates of returns. The main features of the available evidence can be summarized by presenting these rate of returns estimates (see Table 1). Qualifications and inferences will be deferred. Since I shall use it as the standard of comparison for the returns on the various classes of education, I begin with the rate of returns revealed by the U.S. economy. The estimates that follow are all in terms of rates of returns.

[43] I draw here on my paper "The Human Capital Approach to Education" already cited.

U.S. Economy: between 10 and 15 per cent. The implicit rate of returns for the U.S. private domestic economy appears to range between 10 and 15 per cent. These are annual rates, after profits taxes but before personal taxes. They will serve as a benchmark in using the rates that follow as allocative guides.[44] (See Table 1, column 4.)

Elementary Grades: 35 per cent and higher. My estimate made a decade ago, admittedly very rough, places the rate of returns to elementary schooling at about 35 per cent.[45] Hanoch's estimates of the private rates using 1960 census data are, in his language, "extremely high in most cases," mostly above 100 per cent.[46] They confirm the estimates of Hansen.[47] (There may be some upward bias here because of changes in the no-schooling reference class.)

High School: about 25 per cent. High school graduates in Becker's study,[48] restricted to white males, after personal taxes, show a private rate of returns rising from 16 per cent in 1939 to 28 per cent in 1958, and the indication is that it has probably been slightly higher since then.

Quality of Schooling: about 25 per cent. Welch found the rate of returns on improvements in the quality of schooling in rural U.S. farm areas (elementary and high school) to be about 27 per cent.[49] The rate of returns on the expenditure for teachers' salaries as the means of improving the quality of schooling ranged between 23 and 26 per cent.

Nonwhite: rate of returns depressed. The rates of returns on the education of nonwhites, South and North, show less stability than the estimates for whites, and, in general, the estimated rates are lower.[50] Labor market discrimination enters here. Recently, however, the job opportunities for nonwhite college graduates have improved markedly.

College: about 15 per cent. Unlike the upward trend in the rate of returns to high school graduates, college graduates have been earning

[44] D. W. Jorgenson and Zvi Griliches, "The Explanation of Productivity Change," 1967.

[45] Theodore W. Schultz, "Education and Economic Growth," 1961, pp. 78–82.

[46] Giora Hanoch, "Personal Earnings and Investment in Schooling," Ph.D. dissertation, University of Chicago, 1965; also, "An Economic Analysis of Earnings and Schooling," *Journal of Human Resources,* 2, Summer 1967, pp. 310–29.

[47] W. Lee Hansen, "Total and Private Rates of Return to Investment in Schooling," *Journal of Political Economy,* 71, April 1963, pp. 128–40.

[48] Gary S. Becker, *Human Capital: a Theoretical and Empirical Analysis, with Special Reference to Education,* New York, NBER, 1964.

[49] Finis Welch, "Determinants of the Return to Schooling in Rural Farm Areas, 1959," Ph.D. dissertation, University of Chicago, 1966.

[50] Gary S. Becker, *Human Capital,* 1964; and Giora Hanoch, "An Economic Analysis of Earnings and Schooling," 1967.

over the same period in the neighborhood of 15 per cent. This estimate is from Becker's study, which is restricted to white males after personal taxes. (See Table 1.)

Graduate Instruction and Research: about 15 per cent. In estimating the rate of returns on the cost of graduate work much depends on how one treats the stipends that are awarded to graduate students. Treating them as earnings, for which a very plausible case can be made, the rate of returns to graduate work is in the neighborhood of 15 per cent.[51]

In interpreting the estimates for education in Table 1, it must be kept in mind that they are private rates of returns, not social rates; most of them are for white males. They are returns after personal taxes in Becker's study. Note that returns include only the earnings from the particular schooling; thus, the future satisfactions that accrue to the student are not taken into account. The earnings profiles estimates by Hanoch are the best now available. Estimates of educational costs are less satisfactory mainly because of changes in earnings foregone, which have received inadequate attention. Recent work by Mincer [52] shows that the amount and value of the adult training that a person acquires after he enters the labor force depends strongly upon the quantity (and quality) of his education, but no part of this component is credited here to education.

There are difficulties aplenty in estimating the social rates of returns that would be the counterparts of the private rates of returns presented in Table 1. Becker's perceptions of the "social productivity gains" from college suggest that the social and private rates may be quite similar.[53] Hansen's estimates for "total resource investment in schooling" are, in general, similar to his private rates after taxes.[54] But these estimates of social rates of return are subject to serious doubts because of the unsatisfactory state of the underlying concept used in specifying and identifying these rates.[55]

Turning to the inferences to be drawn from these estimates, the inequalities in the private rates of return within the educational enterprise

[51] Theodore W. Schultz, *Investment in Human Capital,* 1971.

[52] Jacob Mincer, "The Distribution of Labor Incomes," 1970.

[53] Gary S. Becker, *Human Capital,* 1964, pp. 117–21.

[54] W. Lee Hansen, "Total and Private Rates of Return to Investment in Schooling," Table 3.

[55] F. K. Hines, Luther Tweeten, and J. Martin Redfern, "Social and Private Rates of Return to Investment in Schooling, by Race-Sex Groups and Regions," *Journal of Human Resources,* Summer 1970, pp. 318–40.

strongly imply that a reallocation of resources is called for. Consider the extreme difference that these estimates reveal between the elementary grades and higher education (college and graduate work), along with the fact that expenditures of public funds on elementary schooling tend to reduce, whereas public funds as they are presently used in higher education may tend to increase, the inequality in the distribution of personal income.[56] Therefore, on both economic efficiency and welfare grounds, a reallocation of public resources in favor of elementary schools is indicated. But are these estimates, admittedly subject to many qualifications, even approximately correct? The answer is in the affirmative; they are broadly consistent with other evidence.

The economic inference at this point is that not enough has been spent on elementary schooling relative to expenditure on higher education. But university administrators, members of school boards, and public officials may look upon the difference in these estimates, regardless of its size, as academic. They know, of course, that virtually every university or college would prefer to shift as large a part of the cost as possible to the state, or better still, to the federal government. But such shifts would merely substitute one source of funds for another. They might contend that elementary school attendance is for all practical purposes universal within the United States. When it comes to investing more to accommodate the growth in enrollment, it is true that elementary school enrollment is leveling off while college enrollment is still rising. It is also true that not all high school graduates who are qualified to enter college and who want to attend are receiving satisfactory instruction. Could it be that the economist is misled by his estimates showing high rates of return to elementary schooling, in the sense that even though they are high, it is in the nature of elementary schooling that they would remain high? Economic thinking provides a strong negative reply. As a matter of fact, there are many ways of spending more on this or that part, that is, on each of the several inputs entering into elementary schooling. Moreover, the economist would point out that for each of these inputs there will be, in all probability, diminishing returns as more of it is brought into play, and that the objective should be to increase the use of each input to the point where the rate of returns on it would be neither higher nor lower than that of the standard of the U.S. economy, say between 10 and 15 per cent.

[56] Barry R. Chiswick, "Human Capital and the Personal Income Distribution by Regions," 1967.

Once we see the heterogeneity of elementary schooling, it will elucidate the investment opportunities. I find it highly plausible to believe, though there are no studies available, that underinvestment in elementary schooling is not characteristic of communities where the level of personal income is high, where the parents are well educated, and where the supply of women who have completed college is large. On the other side of this ledger, there must be many communities and situations where too few resources are allocated to elementary schooling. Among those that qualify, I see the following: (1) rural-farm communities, where people are mostly poor, transport costs large, schools often small, and the salary of teachers unattractive; (2) communities in the rural South, many of them compounded by the racial issue and the poverty of Negroes; (3) some of the other nonwhite populations, e.g., Mexican-Americans throughout the Southwest; (4) the white population of parts of Appalachia and the Piedmont, the people who are left behind; and (5) masses of poor people crowded together in parts of the central cities that lack community stability, where schools are overcrowded, classes inordinately large, and where teaching is done under very adverse circumstances that make it difficult to attract and hold competent, experienced teachers. Thus, considered broadly, these are the parts of the elementary enterprise where underinvestment is most common.

Closely associated with the underinvestment in the elementary grades is the neglect of quality in schooling. It extends also into high school. The combination of school inputs and the amount of them that is required to move to an optimum quality of schooling is still highly speculative in the sense that it has not been subject to the measurement and analysis that is long overdue. Thus, I venture the assumption that it is the competence of the teachers and the grouping of students to maximize their learning motivation that matters most in attaining quality in schooling.

The rate of returns on high school education has continued to rise, notwithstanding the rapid expansion of high school enrollment measured in terms of the proportion of the youth of high school age in high schools. There is undoubtedly much room also here to improve the quality component, but its economic importance is not as clear and plausible as it is in the elementary grades.

The main inference from the rates of returns on college education and graduate instruction and research is that they do not, in general, reveal the underinvestment that comes through so clearly when we examine the elementary grades, high school, and the quality component in schooling. On the one hand, Hanoch's estimates show the rate of returns to graduate instruction as low as 7 per cent, and on the other, the number of earned degrees rose 60 per cent and doctoral degrees, 75 per cent. Thus, there is a puzzle which has led to a reexamination of these estimates. It turns out that the earnings foregone have been reduced substantially by the stipends that graduate students receive, which have all the attributes of earnings rather than income transfers. My estimate of 15 per cent draws on the studies of Stafford and Weiss.[57]

But in planning a program to investigate the general economic efficiency of education, it will be necessary to go beyond the limited knowledge we now have about rates of returns. The interdependency of the various parts of the economy and the critical attributes of capital must become integral parts of such investigations. The condition of any stock of reproducible capital is a product of past investment decisions. It would be rare if such a stock did not reveal some ex post malinvestments because of changes in circumstances that could not have been anticipated at the time the investment decisions were made. Then, too, the condition of any stock of reproducible capital depends on whether it has been properly used, its age, and the depreciation and obsolescence it has been subject to, including the extent to which it contains maldistributions for reasons of the dynamics of the economy. Educational capital is not spared in these respects. The propositions that follow pertain to some of them.

Unemployment Effects.   Educational capital deteriorates when it is kept idle. Thus, unemployment impairs the skills and associated knowledge that a worker has acquired. Physical capital as a rule also deteriorates when it stands idle. But there is a difference, e.g., a fleet of freighters can be placed in "mothballs" for years; a corps of scientists obviously cannot. The consequences of changes in the level of employment also reach into the classroom; they may adversely affect the signals that guide the formation of educational capital. When the level of employment is either appreciably below or above normal, it distorts and impairs the information that students and schools require for making efficient allocative decisions with regard to education.

[57] Frank P. Stafford, "Graduate Student Income and Consumption," Ph.D. dissertation, Graduate School of Business, University of Chicago, 1968; Yoram Weiss, "Allocation of Time and Occupational Choice," Ph.D. dissertation, Stanford University, 1968. The puzzle is resolved in Chapter 7 of my *Investment in Human Capital,* 1971.

Productive Life of Educational Capital.[58]   None of it lasts beyond the death of the individual who has it. But unlike the wonderful "one-hoss shay," the productive life of educational capital typically does not go to pieces all at once. It depreciates along the way, it becomes obsolete, it is altered by changes in retirement and by the state of employment. The one-hoss shay model, with no depreciation, no obsolescence, and then sudden death, will not do. Although knowledge about these processes is still meager, it is clear that one of the critical problems is the high rate of obsolescence of much of our educational capital. Changes in the demand for skills are an obvious attribute of our type of economic growth. New techniques of production require new skills, and old skills become obsolete. It should be possible to develop programs of instruction that would provide additional flexibility in the ability of the student to reform and renew his skills in adjusting to the changes in the demand for them. Although the optimum combination of specialized and general instruction is an unsettled issue, what is becoming increasingly clear is that the higher the level and the better the quality of the education that a student obtains, the more he will invest and gain from on-the-job training after he has completed his formal schooling, as Mincer has shown.[59] Training for specific jobs, including a wide array of highly specialized skills, should be postponed in general. In addition to on-the-job training, there are efficient adult learning arrangements. Going up the scale in gaining flexibility, knowledge pertaining to principles and theories in all probability reduces this rate of obsolescence. In my thinking, the highest priority should be given to instruction devoted to problem solving, learning how to bring established knowledge to bear and how to use analytical methods in solving problems.

Distribution of Educational Capital.   The existing stock of educational capital in the United States reveals many different types of distribution. The classes of distribution that await economic investigation are those that imply malinvestment and that can be put to an economic test.

[58] See Yoram Ben-Porath, "The Production of Human Capital and the Life Cycle of Earnings," *Journal of Political Economy,* 75, August 1967, pp. 352–65, and, importantly, his "Some Aspects of the Life Cycle of Earnings," Ph.D. dissertation, Harvard University, 1967; see also Sherwin Rosen, "Knowledge, Obsolescence and Income," University of Rochester and National Bureau of Economic Research, November 1970, unpublished.

[59] Jacob Mincer, "On-the-Job Training: Costs, Returns, and Some Implications," *Journal of Political Economy,* 70, October 1962, supplement, pp. 50–79; and "The Distribution of Labor Incomes," 1970.

Investment in education is heavily weighted in favor of youth. The fact that schooling costs less when one is young and renders satisfactions and earnings for a longer period gives youth a strong comparative advantage. Thus, there are compelling economic reasons for schooling to be acquired early in life. Then, too, as a result of the marked secular rise in the level of schooling, young people enter the labor force with more educational capital than earlier generations had when they started to work. Thus, the personal distribution of educational capital by age of worker is strongly skewed toward youth. But from an investment point of view, this secular advantage of youth is no indication that there has been a malinvestment. Youth has still another advantage, but the gains from it are in part acquired at the expense of older workers. The advances in knowledge become an integral part of instruction and as this occurs, they are the source of new skills. But these new skills tend to make the skills of older workers obsolete. It would be very convenient if workers with obsolete educational capital (skills) could be abandoned like obsolete physical capital! But this option is foreclosed on welfare grounds. Much remains to be done in clarifying policy choices in solving this problem of gains and losses.[60]

No small part of the inequality in the distribution of schooling arises from the inequality in the distribution of personal income. Children of poor people acquire not only somewhat less schooling but, what is much more important, the schooling they obtain is, as a rule, much lower in quality than that acquired by children of families (in communities) with high incomes. There have been some useful reforms in local and state finance. Bringing the capital market into play to provide the necessary additional resources where people are poor is not solving this problem. Tax-exempt school bonds are not the solution. The fact of the matter is that schooling is neither free nor equal. The two common expressions, "free public schooling" and "equal educational opportunities," are in this context empty phrases. Schooling is inescapably an expensive enterprise, privately and publicly. The term "opportunities" is most ambiguous. Nevertheless, as already noted, the policy implications of the inequality in schooling that is associated with the inequality in the distribution of personal income are strong and clear. *Relatively more of the investment resources entering into education should be allocated purely on economic efficiency grounds in favor of the children from poor homes.*

[60] Theodore W. Schultz, "Our Welfare State and the Welfare of Farm People," *Social Service Review,* 38, June 1964, pp. 123–29.

As already noted, the condition of the stock of educational capital is adversely affected by an overemphasis on quantity of schooling relative to the emphasis given to its quality. In quantitative terms, looking at days of school attendance per year, there has been a marked rise in attendance in elementary and high schools. At the turn of the century, for the country as a whole, the average number of days was ninety-nine. It is now in the neighborhood of 160, where it has leveled off. Furthermore, there has been a marked reduction in the differences in days of school attendance on the part of pupils in different parts of the United States. *But the differences in the quality of schooling are great, and they are the heart of one of our most serious problems, especially so in elementary schooling.* It is in terms of quality that many rural children and many children from the homes of nonwhite families are at a marked disadvantage.

Another view of education is its distribution between higher education on the one hand and elementary and secondary schooling on the other. The underinvestment in elementary and perhaps also in secondary schooling relative to that entering into higher education is undoubtedly in large part a result of the way we have financed education. The part of higher education that is dependent upon public revenue has developed mainly with the growth of the land grant universities. They are state universities, largely supported by revenue from the state, although the amount of federal funds has become increasingly important. Elementary and high schools started as local enterprises, and the progress in enlarging the financial base of these schools has been a difficult institutional reform. Granting federal funds in any significant amounts to support these schools is a very recent development. The unequal distribution of personal income already discussed is part of the explanation of this problem. The differences between regions, with the South lagging behind, and the particular effects that economic growth has had upon some economic sectors, notably the adverse effects on the size of the agricultural population, are also a part of the explanation.

Tied Women.   In marriage, as a rule, the woman, regardless of her education, is bound in seeking a job appropriate to her skills to the location where her husband works. Suppose the cultural rules were to designate the woman as the head of the household, with her job opportunity determining the location of work of the family! The man would then be compelled to adjust his lot to this turn in circumstances. For women, it would imply that the incentives to acquire a higher education, including advanced professional degrees, would be vastly enhanced. Major metropolitan centers tend to reduce this constraint that marriage imposes upon the woman as she seeks to enter the labor force.[61] It is most severe in a strictly rural or farming area.

One of the major omissions in the studies of human capital is the investment in the education of women.[62] One might conclude that human capital is the unique property of the male population! If so, we would do well to drop the term "human capital" and replace it with "male capital." It would serve notice that human capital is sex-specific! Despite all of the schooling of females and other expenditures on them, they appear to be of no account in the accounting of human capital. If females are capital-free, in view of all that is spent on them, we are in real trouble analytically, unless we can show that it is purely for current consumption. There is no way of hiding the fact that females attend elementary and high school to the same extent as males and probably perform a bit better than males. In college attendance they fall behind somewhat; of the 4.9 million enrolled in October 1966, about two-fifths were women. Even so, in terms of median years of school completed, of all persons twenty-five years and older in the United States, females are slightly ahead of males and the difference in favor of females has been increasing over time. Surely, it cannot be denied that the cost of all this schooling of females is real and large. Nor is it plausible that all of these direct and indirect costs are only for current consumption. The investment component must be large. But if there is little to show for it, how do we patch up the economic behavioral assumption underlying the investment in education?

Mincer and Becker have each devoted a couple of pages to women. Mincer found that on-the-job training is not for women.[63] Becker observes that the rate of returns to female college graduates may not be lower than for males "because direct costs are somewhat lower and opportunity costs are much lower for women." [64] But differential earnings are a small part of the story. The main reason for the failure to get at the returns on women's schooling has been the long neglect of any accounting of the economic value of the nonmarket activities that center in the household.

[61] Glen G. Cain, *Married Women in the Labor Force,* Chicago, University of Chicago Press, 1966; and Jacob Mincer, "Labor Force Participation of Married Women," *Aspects of Labor Economics,* H. Gregg Lewis (ed.), Universities–National Bureau Conference, 14, Princeton University Press for NBER, 1962.

[62] I draw here on my "The Reckoning of Education as Human Capital," in *Education, Income, and Human Capital,* W. Lee Hansen (ed.), New York, NBER, 1970, pp. 297–306.

[63] Jacob Mincer, "On-the-Job Training," 1962, pp. 66–68.

[64] Gary S. Becker, *Human Capital,* 1964, pp. 100–102.

Furthermore, there are many puzzles about the economic behavior of women that can be resolved once their human capital is taken into account. Young females leave the better parts of agriculture more readily than young males; these females have a schooling advantage and they are not held back by any specific on-the-farm training as are males. The explanation of the preponderance of women in most Negro colleges before school integration is to be found in the differences between the job opportunities open to Negro women and Negro men graduates. At a more general level, there is the slow, yet real, economic emancipation of women. It may be viewed as a consequence of growth and affluence.[65] But a part of this rise in family affluence is some function of the rise in the education of women, to a far larger degree than is revealed by the increasing participation of women in the labor force. Most of the benefits from the education of women are realized at the micro level of the household as a consequence of the increases in the effectiveness and efficiency associated with the rise in the education of women.

Job and School Discrimination.   The adverse effects of racial and religious discrimination on the availability of jobs, on wages and salaries, and on education are measurable, and recent research provides firm estimates in this area. It is also evident from our recent history how difficult it is to free the job market and the educational enterprise from the adverse effects of the social virus of discrimination, which is so deeply embedded in the individual preferences that account for the discriminatory behavior. The effects of discrimination upon the personal distribution of the existing stock of educational capital is an open record; the professions have not been free of it; and employment in the crafts and building trades is plagued with it. But it is the Negro in the rural South who is burdened with the worst of the consequences of job and school discrimination. The studies by Welch on the effects of discrimination upon the Negro in the rural South strongly supports this inference.[66] The hindrances to the free choice of professions and the role that professional associations and governmental agencies play, with major attention to the medical profession, are shown by Friedman and Kuznets in the first study

[65] Harry G. Johnson, "Economic Theory and Contemporary Society," *University of Toronto Quarterly,* 37, July 1968, pp. 321–37.

[66] Finis Welch, "Measurement of the Quality of Schooling," *American Economic Review,* 56, May 1966, pp. 379–92; also his "Labor-Market Discrimination: An Interpretation of Income Differences in the Rural South," *Journal of Political Economy,* 75, June 1967, pp. 225–40.

of this type. [67] An approach that brings economics to bear more generally has been developed by Becker in his *The Economics of Discrimination*.[68]

The malinvestment in education that is a consequence of discrimination is of two major parts. First, students and their families who are subject to discrimination will have less of an economic incentive to acquire the amount and quality of schooling that they would were they free from discrimination. Thus, there is an underinvestment for them. Consider the following. White students attending high school are aware, as are their parents, that the additional earnings associated with the completion of high school are likely to bring them a 25 per cent rate of return on the additional cost of the high school education. Suppose also that, because of job discrimination, Negro high school students are aware, as are their parents, that the completion of high school will not improve their earnings, and that for them the rate of return on the additional cost of attending and completing high school will be zero. Under such circumstances, we would expect—and we also find—that white students in general give a high priority to completing high school. For Negroes we would expect the opposite to be true. The evidence is mixed because there are substantial differences in costs and in the rates of return, depending upon where they are located and associated circumstances. *It is only a small step from the above to the differences in motivation for attending and performing well while in school.* The inference is that an important part of the observed differences in motivation between white and Negro students is a consequence of job discrimination against Negroes.

Table 2, which follows, shows that the difference in income between Southern white and nonwhite rural farm males who were twenty-

[67] Milton Friedman and Simon Kuznets, *Income from Independent Professional Practice,* New York, NBER, 1945.

[68] Gary S. Becker, *The Economics of Discrimination,* second ed., Chicago, University of Chicago Press, 1971.

Other recent studies are: Harold Demsetz, "Minorities in the Market Place," *North Carolina Law Review,* 43, February 1965, pp. 272–97; Harry J. Gilman, "Economic Discrimination and Unemployment," *American Economic Review,* 55, December 1965, pp. 1077–96; Anne O. Krueger, "The Economics of Discrimination," *Journal of Political Economy,* 71, October 1963, pp. 481–86; William M. Landes, "The Economics of Fair Employment Laws," *Journal of Political Economy,* 76, July/August 1968, pp. 507–52; David William Rasmussen, "The Determinants of the Non-White/White Income Ratio," Ph.D. dissertation, St. Louis, Washington University, 1969; Lester C. Thurow, *Poverty and Discrimination,* Washington, D.C., Brookings Institution, 1969.

TABLE 2

Estimated Impact on Nonwhite Income of Market
Discrimination and Inferior Quality of Schooling

	Years of Schooling Completed		
	5–7	8	12
Income			
White	$2,090	$2,340	$3,790
Nonwhite	1,300	1,480	1,840
Difference	790	860	1,950
1. Impact of market discrimination			
against physical labor	250	250	250
2. Impact of discrimination against			
schooling [a]	540	610	1,700
(a) Inferior quality of schooling	200	230	630
(b) Market discrimination against			
education	340	380	1,070

Source: Finis Welch, "Labor-Market Discrimination: An Interpretation of Income Differences in the Rural South," *Journal of Political Economy,* 15, June 1967, Table 5, p. 239.

[a] The adjustment for interaction between quality of schooling and market discrimination against education is prorated according to the proportion of the total (difference in the return to schooling) accounted for by each. Actually, interaction represents 14 per cent of the total discrimination against schooling.

five years old or over in 1959 was $790 for those who had completed five to seven years and $1,950 for those who had completed twelve years of schooling. For those with the least schooling, about one-third of the difference in income is attributed to market discrimination against physical labor per se; two-thirds is attributed to market discrimination against schooling. For those with twelve years of schooling, the absolute value of the estimate of the market discrimination against physical labor is no larger than it was for those with the least schooling. It accounts for little more than one-eighth of the difference in income. Thus, by all odds, the major part of the difference in income is attributed to discrimination against schooling. Welch separates the latter component into two parts: One is associated with the inferior quality of schooling, which accounted for $200 of the difference for those with the least schooling and $630 for those with twelve years of schooling. The other part, namely market discrimination against education (in the language of Welch), predominates with $340 for the group with the least schooling and rises markedly for those with twelve years of schooling, where $1,070 is attributed to the discrimination against this level of education.

It is appropriate to quote the policy implications that Welch has drawn from his findings:

> It would seem that discriminatory quality of schooling is more easily eliminated than market discrimination, because legislative authorities have relatively little control over such markets. In fact, to the extent that market discrimination is determined largely by sociological phenomena, we cannot expect these factors to be eliminated either quickly or easily. Nevertheless, the elimination of discrimination in quality of schooling may be an important vehicle for removing income differences; for an improvement in the quality of schooling will: (1) reduce the observed discrimination against schooling, (2) induce an increased investment in schooling, and (3) induce greater effort while in school, which will increase the quantity of education per unit of attendance time. In addition, the reduction of differences in education may reduce associational friction, which then reduces discrimination.[69]

Capital Market.   Would that the capital market could serve students who require funds to invest in their education as effectively as it does those who are engaged in the formation of physical capital. The difference, so it seems to me, is large. It is not simply a matter of imperfections in the capital market as it serves students. The difference in the legal foundations of property and of the rights of persons are a major part of the explanation. In the domain of physical capital, the suppliers of investment funds function within well-established institutions which rest on the rights of property. Funds that enter into the formation of human capital, regardless of the form it takes, do not have the legal status of property. As part of the person, educational capital is subject to the rights of persons and these rights are not tailored to enhance the economic efficiency of the capital market.

There is room, nevertheless, for improvement in the capital market serving students. A good deal of experience is being accumulated from different approaches in providing loans to students, both on private and public account. It is undoubtedly true that extending long-term loans to students, which is what is called for, will play an increasing role in

[69] Finis Welch, "Labor-Market Discrimination," 1967, pp. 239–40.

financing higher education in the years to come. Where the family has tangible assets, property of value, the use of such assets as collateral would not be a departure from traditional capital market experience. Loans that rest on the level of the income stream of the family are a development that is still in its infancy. But with the relatively high level of income of so large a part of U.S. families, it carries considerable promise. In part, it will be necessary to rid our social mores from some convenient clichés, honorable as they may appear. The one that is pure fancy occurs frequently when students apply for financial aid from the university. They have taken a private vow that they must now be financially independent of their parents. How convenient! Although many of them reveal that the income of their parents is surprisingly high, it does not occur to them that this declaration of financial independence is self-serving in their plea for financial aid from the university, in a context where the higher education will add to their earnings and thus, if the aid is granted, promises to increase the inequality in the distribution of personal income in society.[70]

Tax Laws. The unequal treatment of physical and human capital by our tax laws is another source of inefficiency in the allocation of investment resources to education. As already noted, educational capital, like reproducible physical capital, is subject to depreciation and obsolescence. The established tax treatment takes account of both depreciation and obsolescence in the case of physical capital, but this accounting is not extended to educational capital. Although earnings foregone while attending school do not enter into taxable income, none of the direct private cost of education is treated as capital in our tax laws. In brief, our tax laws, including the extension from time to time of investment credits, appear to be all but blind to the fact that educational capital entails maintenance and depreciation, becomes obsolete, and disappears at death. More equal treatment with respect to each of these factors would enhance the investment priorities in education relative to investment in physical capital forms.

Incentives and Information. When it comes to making optimum allocative decisions pertaining to the investment in education, the system of incentives is weak and the state of information in bad repair at many points. This situation accounts for many inefficiencies in the way invest-

[70] The problem of financing, pricing, and supplying the instruction of higher education is exceedingly complex. See my paper "The Optimal Investment in College Instruction: Equity and Efficiency" in the supplement to the *Journal of Political Economy,* May/June 1972.

ment resources are allocated in this area. But who should make these allocative decisions? Who is best qualified? One strongly held view is that students and their families are best qualified. Those who hold this view appeal to consumer sovereignty and thus to the private self-interest of students (and their families). There is another view that contends that there are substantial external economies or social benefits that accrue not to the student, but to others in society, and that therefore these allocative decisions can best be made by public or other social bodies. What is the contribution of school administrators in managing our complex educational enterprise? In view of the inefficiencies that are consequences of poor incentives and poor information, the effect of these on the decisions of students, teachers, administrators, and public bodies requires a brief comment.

The key to student sovereignty is the private self-interests of students and of their families. Their self-interest should be sufficient to bring about an efficient allocation of investment resources to education privately under the following conditions: [71] (1) competition in producing educational services along with efficient prices of these services; (2) availability of optimal information to students; (3) efficient capital market serving students; and (4) no appreciable disassociation of private and social benefits (losses) from education.

A clear view of the function of the private self-interests of students in these allocative decisions is blurred by arguments about the underlying conditions. Surely it is possible to have competitive pricing of educational services. As noted above, student loans from public and private sources can be devised to provide additional capital. It should also be possible to take account of social benefits (losses). Nor is the Achilles' heel of student sovereignty in the domain of information,[72] although the long standing controversy over this issue is still with us, as it was when the classical economists divided on this point.[73]

The following quotation summarizes the underlying issues inherent in the student sovereignty approach: [74]

[71] Theodore W. Schultz, "Resources for Higher Education: An Economist's View," *Journal of Political Economy,* 76, May/June 1968, pp. 327–47.

[72] Richard B. Freeman (see footnote 15) provides strong evidence that college students are surprisingly well-informed about job opportunities.

[73] E. G. West, "Private Versus Public Education," *Journal of Political Economy,* 72, October 1964, pp. 465–75.

[74] Theodore W. Schultz, "Resources for Higher Education," p. 342; also in *Investment in Human Capital,* 1971, Chapter 10.

In enlarging the scope and improving the performance of student sovereignty in allocating resources to . . . education, the gaps in information and the distortions in incentives really matter. On earnings foregone, students are well-informed, but on their capabilities as students they are in doubt. With regard to the benefits that will accrue to them, the state of information is far from optimum. But much worse still is the lack of information on the differences in the quality of the educational services of different colleges and universities. Nowhere are students confronted by prices for these services that are equal to the real cost of producing them, and therefore the prices to which they respond are not socially efficient prices. As a consequence, no matter how efficient students are privately in their decisions, from the point of view of the economy as a whole, the allocation of resources to . . . education will not be socially efficient.

Turning to policy implications, the ideal price for the educational services that students obtain should be neither more nor less than the real cost of producing these services. This proposition, however, does not support the view that there should be no difference between public and private tuition, or, for that matter, among public or private schools. Equality of tuition would merely replace one type of price distortion by another type because it would conceal the differences in the quality of educational services provided by different schools. The policy implications pertaining to the capital market have been discussed. Thus, we come to the task of improving the state of information. A major step in accomplishing this task is the development of socially efficient prices to which the students can respond. But more than this is required. They must know what they are buying. Specifications that are only in quantitative terms are not sufficient. Much depends upon knowing the differences in the quality of the educational services. Truth in advertising is an approach that might well be applied to the materials that schools make available and especially so to the catalogues that universities issue.

3. Postschool Investment in Human Capital

As a first approximation of the economic importance of on-the-job training, we come to Mincer's 1962 paper. His estimates of this form of investment that males in the U.S. labor force made in themselves came to $5.7 billion during 1939 and to $12.5 billion in 1958, both in 1954 dollars.[75] Using Mincer's figures, my estimate of the stock of capital embodied in males in the labor force from their investment in on-the-job training as of 1957 came to $347 billion, compared to the educational stock of capital in the labor force at that time of $535 billion.[76] Meanwhile, Mincer and others have extended both the theoretical and empirical parts of this work.[77]

The complementarity between education and postschool investment is firmly established. A general earnings function that includes not only education but also postschool investment is at hand. But the state of the economic efficiency and that of the equity associated with the various forms of postschool investment are still among the unknowns.

4. Preschool Investment in Human Capital

National concern about the unequal start among children when they enter upon their regular schooling appears once again to be at a low ebb. At the launching of the "headstart" programs to reduce this inequality, the contributions that these programs were expected to make became grossly exaggerated. These expectations could not be realized.[78] The heterogeneity of the home inputs characterizing the families with children who receive a bad start and that of the communities in which they reside has made and will continue to make it exceedingly difficult to design programs appropriate to the task. Measurement of the results have been plagued by no end of problems pertaining to data, method, and the precise purpose of these programs.

Despite these trials and errors, there are strong reasons for believing that preschool investment ranks high, even higher than that pertaining to elementary schooling, both in terms of rates of return and of equity. It is obvious that there are no earnings foregone from the value of the time of the children at the preschool level. The required investment must be made in large part by motivating the mothers of the children who are reared in homes beset with disadvantages, and by enhancing the ability of these mothers to give their children a better start than they are now capable of doing. Thus, it becomes a dual investment, for it is a means of

[75] Jacob Mincer, "On-the-Job Training," Table 2.

[76] Theodore W. Schultz, "Reflections on Investment in Man," Table 1, p. 6.

[77] Jacob Mincer, "On-the-Job Training"; his 1970 survey is an excellent accounting of this progress and its implications for research.

[78] For some evidence on this issue, see Thomas I. Ribich, *Education and Poverty*, Washington, D.C., Brookings Institution, 1968.

increasing the skills and knowledge of mothers with low levels of schooling and, at the same time, through them, those of their children.[79]

In view of the economic disequilibria that characterize the schooling enterprises in the United States at this juncture in our history, I expect that preschool investments will prove to be a consistent extension of the rates of return profile associated with schooling in the following sense: The rates of return will turn out to be highest for the preschool endeavors once efficient ways of making them are discovered.

5. Human Capital Approach to Migration

In policy there is a clear distinction between migration among nations and that within the nation. In economic analysis, however, the human capital approach is applicable to both classes of migration, and substantial contributions have already been made to both classes. But I shall restrict my comments to internal migration.[80] It performs an important economic function in a modern economy where there is sustained economic growth, and especially so in a large and diverse country such as the United States. The dynamics of the economy are constantly changing the demand for skills and the distribution of the demand for human agents among farming areas, metropolitan areas, and regions. In addition, as personal incomes rise, more and more people, especially so as they approach retirement, migrate to take advantage of consumption opportunities that are associated with differences in climate. Whether in response to better job opportunities or to better consumption opportunities, the migration is not costless. Since it entails both costs and returns, it is appropriate to treat it as an investment in man.

I find it hard to explain why policy and public programs in the United States have failed to come to grips with the problem of internal migration in view of its importance and the advances in economic knowledge pertaining to it. It could, of course, be argued that we have a laissez-faire policy and that the magnitude of the mobility of American people based on millions of private decisions provides strong support

[79] Jacob Mincer has called my attention to the study by D. J. Dugan "The Impact of Parental and Educational Investment Upon School Achievement," *Proceedings of the Social Statistics Section,* American Statistical Association, 1969.

[80] The state of the work in economics pertaining to the migration among countries has been broadly reviewed in a recent paper by Anthony Scott "The Brain Drain—Is a Human-Capital Approach Justified?" in *Education, Income, and Human Capital,* W. Lee Hansen (ed.), New York, NBER, 1970. An important part of the recent literature is addressed to the "brain drain."

for this policy. The reply to this argument is of two parts: (1) Given the information available to people privately, no matter how efficient their private decisions may be with respect to migrating, their decisions will not necessarily be socially efficient in view of the effects of migration on the economic system, because of the interdependency of its various parts, which entails effects going beyond their private calculus; and (2) our policy is not truly a laissez-faire policy—public expenditures on schooling and higher education, on adult training, and on science and the development of technology, to mention only the more obvious ones, have strong measurable effects on internal migration. My judgment on this issue has undoubtedly been much influenced by the economic absurdities that characterize U.S. agricultural programs. The economic dynamics of agriculture has greatly reduced the job opportunities in that area. The farm population has declined from thirty to less than ten million during recent decades. But this massive migration has not received a shred of assistance in terms of information to guide private decisions or of financial aid to cover some of the cost of the migration, despite the fact that billions of dollars of public funds are appropriated annually to finance the agricultural programs, and despite the fact that these programs have accentuated the out-migration, which in turn has compounded the urban problem.

While the policy demand for economic information pertaining to migration is wanting, the supply has benefited from the application of the human capital approach. The central hypothesis is that the act of migrating is an investment and that the lifetime expected returns associated with the differences in job opportunities among labor markets or in consumption opportunities among locations as places to live determine the alternative investment opportunities pertaining to migration. Sjaastad, following his Ph.D. research, set the stage for this approach in his 1962 paper.[81]

Schwartz found that differentials in lifetime earnings provide a better explanation of migration than differentials in current earnings, and that the response to the differences in lifetime earnings is lowest for the least educated persons and increases monotonically with education.[82]

[81] Larry A. Sjaastad, "Income and Migration in the United States," Ph.D. dissertation, University of Chicago, 1961; also his "The Costs and Returns of Human Migration," *Journal of Political Economy,* 70, October 1962, supplement, pp. 80–93.

[82] Aba Schwartz, "Migration and Lifetime Earnings in the U.S.," Ph.D. dissertation, University of Chicago, 1968.

His findings are consistent with the hypothesis that one of the effects of education is to reduce the cost of obtaining information about job opportunities. He also found that a high ratio of gross to net migration is a result of aggregation rather than a consequence of inefficiency inherent in the process of migration.

The O'Neill study is an additional advance analytically, for it takes into account explicitly the effects of consumption opportunities upon migration.[83] Her model and empirical work encompass not only labor market job opportunities but also the differences in the effects of "destination" and the "origin" income on the value of income in consumption. She succeeds in resolving a variety of puzzling questions on economic behavior associated with migration.

Research possibilities with respect to migration are excellent both in terms of theory and data. There are also some favorable signs that the search for a meaningful migration policy is under way in the public domain. The private demand for information about alternative investment opportunities in migration is strong and clear.

6. Health as an Investment

The large private and public expenditures related to health and the maze of unsettled economic questions in this area argue for the establishment of a National Bureau of Economic Health Research! Although problems of economic efficiency and equity abound in the allocation of resources to health, economic investigations are not only sparse but also either mainly in research units partial to the purposes of particular health programs or still in the cottage industry stage at the fringes of academic work in economics. It is hard to avoid the conclusion that, given the resources now devoted to economic research in the United States, the neglect of the economic problems in health represents a serious malallocation of even these resources.

The endeavor to establish "better health and less illness" as a social goal is fruitless in determining how much should be spent on any one of the many health programs relative to other programs or relative to all alternative opportunities that call for resources. There is obviously a preference for health that is revealed in the demand for it. It is also obvious that the activities that account for the supply of health services are

[83] June O'Neill, "The Effects of Income and Education on Inter-Regional Migration," Ph.D. dissertation, Columbia University, 1969.

costly.[84] Many of the acquired attributes of health have durability, and, to the extent they do, their acquisition represents an investment in human beings, as Mushkin made clear in her 1962 paper.[85]

Moreover, the demand for economic information pertaining to health is not wanting. It is highly visible in all manner of public and private questions that are not being answered. Why does the price of medical services rise so much more than the rest of the consumer price index? Why does the supply of medical personnel not increase more rapidly in view of the high salaries doctors receive for their services? [86] What accounts for the serious trouble besetting the national programs of Medicare and Medicaid? Would an all-inclusive national health insurance program provide a solution to these problems? These questions, and there are many more, raise fundamental economic issues that await analyses.

Solutions for these issues are not to be had by concentrating on investigations to explain the differences in observed mortality, nor by attempting to account for differences in perceptions and attitudes toward health on the part of different classes of people. It is not in the domain of economic analysis to explain tastes or preferences for health. Leaving aside the more aggregative effects of health programs upon illness, lost work days for reasons of sickness, and private expenditures on health services, as well as the effects of inadequate diets and the consumption of cigarettes and drugs, what is called for above all else are the theoretical advances and empirical applications of the new extensions of consumer theory, an approach that concentrates on households, treating them as active producers of a wide array of objects that are an integral part of consumer choice. The only study known to me that uses this approach to get at the economic problem of health is that by Grossman.[87] He treats "good health" as a durable component and then proceeds to investigate the acquisition of "health capital" as one component in human capital.

[84] NBER's studies pertaining to the economics of health are clarifying the various supply and demand components. Reports are becoming available by Victor R. Fuchs and associates, and are reviewed in the last two annual reports of NBER. A volume entitled *Economics of Health and Medical Care* is forthcoming.

[85] Selma J. Mushkin, "Health as an Investment," *Journal of Political Economy*, 70, October 1962, supplement, pp. 129–57.

[86] The study by Milton Friedman and Simon Kuznets *Income from Independent Professional Practice,* 1945, stands as a pioneering work in applying the rate of return concept to the investment in human capital restricted to this class of high professional skills.

[87] Michael Grossman, "The Demand for Health: A Theoretical and Empirical Investigation," Ph.D. dissertation, Columbia University, 1969.

He assumes that the members of the household inherit an initial stock of health which depreciates over time, usually at an increasing rate, at least after some stage in the life cycle, and that the life cycle can be made somewhat longer by means of investment. The analysis then proceeds to the observable inputs that account for the investments in the stock of health via medical care, own time, diets, recreation, and other market goods. The implicit production function also depends on the identifiable environmental variables that alter the efficiency of the household in this process, the most important of which is the level of education of the members of the household.[88]

7. The Search for Information

Complete and perfect information in making private and public decisions has long been a convenient assumption in economics. Economic analysis, however, has paid a high price for this assumption, for it conceals the effects of a major component in all economic transactions. Stigler brought this issue to a head in a classic paper "The Economics of Information." [89] In applying his approach to information in the labor market, Stigler argues: [90]

> Even with strict homogeneity of commodities, we usually find some dispersion in the prices which are offered by sellers or buyers. Only if either buyers have complete knowledge of all sellers' offers, or all sellers have complete knowledge of all buyers' offers, will there be a single price. Complete knowledge, however, is seldom possessed, simply because it costs more to learn the alternative prices than (at the margin) this information yields.

That meaningful results can be obtained in analyzing the search by workers when they enter the labor force is clear from Stigler's empirical analysis in the same article, restricted to the graduates of the Graduate School of Business at the University of Chicago in 1960 and 1961.

The heart of the information problem is expressed by Professor Johnson as follows: [91]

[88] See Michael Grossman's Department of Economics Workshop paper, University of Chicago, 1970, which carries the same title as his Ph.D. dissertation cited above; see also NBER's *50th Annual Report,* September 1970, pp. 93–95.

[89] *Journal of Political Economy,* June 1961.

[90] George J. Stigler, "Information in the Labor Market," *Journal of Political Economy,* 70, October 1962, supplement, pp. 94–105.

[91] Harry G. Johnson, "The Economic Approach to Social Questions," 1968, p. 10.

The practice of economizing on the acquisition and dissemination of relevant information is at least as characteristic of political as it is of economic activity. The fact that decisions are so frequently taken in this sort of way is generally regarded in the neo-classical tradition of economic theory, in which knowledge is assumed to be costless, as a reflection of the irrationality, or gullibility-cum-rapacity, of man in a capitalist economic system; it is, on the contrary, a manifestation of rationality in a situation in which the decisions that have to be taken are increasingly numerous, multiplying as incomes rise, while time is short and increasingly valuable. Two important implications for social questions are that the production and distribution of information relevant to consumption choices is a necessary part of the activities of the economic system, not merely a wasteful excrescence of it; and that the economizing process will ensure that information is provided and acted on in a form falling far short of the standard that would be exacted by academic scholarship.

This acquisition of information can be viewed as an integral part of postschool investment in human capital discussed under (4) above. But there is much to be said for looking upon it as a separate area because of the pervasiveness of the problem of information in all manner of economic transactions. The economics of information is indeed seminal in its implications. As a research area, it still is in its infancy, awaiting exploration despite the rewarding research opportunities it offers.

8. Fertility, Children, and Population: A New Economic Approach

It is hard not to become mesmerized into believing the macro population projections. Paul Ehrlich's profitable *Population Bomb,* with people behaving like fruitflies, leaves little time before it will be doomsday. But the social behavior of parents in bearing and rearing children remains in large part unknown. However fancy the macro population projections may be, they are statistical artifacts, for there is no received theory that accounts for the behavior changes over time of any given population or for that among different populations, although demographers have made much progress in standardizing and in treating the complex components that characterize demographic data. Suffice it to say for the purpose at hand that traditional economic theory is not capable of explaining the observed diversity and changes in population growth. Moreover, odd as it may seem in view of the plethora of economic growth models, none has been successful in analyzing changes in the population as an endogenous variable in economic growth.

It is obvious that recent marked declines in death rates throughout much of the world are a factor in population growth, that poor people tend to have the most children, that modern contraceptive techniques are in demand, and that the rise in the value of women's time reduces the size of families. But what is not obvious is that children are a form of human capital from which parents derive satisfactions and services, and that the bearing and rearing of children entail sacrifices consisting of the parents' own time, of market commodities, and of public services. Thus, it would appear that parents (society, too), in acquiring these future satisfactions and services from children, are making allocative choices that are in principle economic decisions.

It is undoubtedly true that many thoughtful people will be offended by this economic approach of treating children as human capital. It would appear to debase the family and motherhood. Moreover, these highly personal activities of parents would seem to be far beyond the realm of the market-oriented economic calculus. I repeatedly expressed the same concern about these issues when I began to apply the concept of human capital to education. It, too, could be viewed as debasing the cultural purposes of education. I pointed out with care and at length that education as human capital was fully consistent with serving cultural purposes in acquiring future satisfactions and earnings associated with schooling and higher education. The same basic logic is applicable in an attempt to explain the sacrifices that parents make in acquiring satisfactions and services derived from their children.

It could, of course, be argued that parents are indifferent to any and all economic considerations when it comes to having children. I shall not, at this point, enter upon the reasons for not accepting this line of argument. I shall, instead, proceed on the proposition that parents are not indifferent with respect to the number of children they want and in fact bear and rear. I shall assume that parents value their children because they acquire satisfaction from them and under many circumstances also obtain some productive services from them in the home and from the work they do outside of the home—as well as, in many parts of the world, some old age security in having food and shelter when they, the parents, are no longer able to provide for themselves because of old age. Truly, for most of the people of the world, *children are the poor man's capital,* on which he is dependent during his declining years. This particular fact of life probably holds the key to the most critical part of the world's population problem. But to proceed with the approach advanced here, I take it to be true that whatever benefits parents derive from their children, these benefits entail two sorts of costs: the opportunity cost of the parents' time, predominantly that of the woman, in having and rearing a child, and the cost of commodities and services in the form of food, clothes, shelter, health care, and the schooling of the child. The central behavioral proposition is that parents tend to equalize these benefits and costs. It is obvious, of course, that this proposition implies that parents do not behave like robots in having children. Nor do they breed like fruitflies up to the limit of their food supply.

I have already alluded to the fact that most of the people of the world are very poor and that children are the poor man's capital on which parents are dependent when they can no longer provide for themselves. But whether they are poor or rich, the social and economic characteristics of the community whose members they are systematically affect the costs and benefits of having children. The subjective and pecuniary costs encompass (1) the opportunity cost of the woman's time, (2) the value of child labor, (3) family income, (4) education, (5) institutions, and (6) contraception information and techniques. The demand of parents for children with respect to both numbers and quality (e.g., investment in the child's health and schooling) is clear and cogent from the recent studies of the micro economics of the household.

The new economic approach to fertility, children, and population has been made possible by the extensions in economic theory already presented in some detail in part II of this survey. The foundation of this approach is provided by the development of the concept of human capital and the extension of theory to deal with the allocation of time. In large measure, it has been the conceptualization of the allocation of time that has led to a wide array of empirical studies concentrating on the nonmarket activities of the household in acquiring market commodities, in processing them, and in consuming them, including the allocation of time and of commodities and services in bearing and rearing children.

Foreshadowing this approach was Becker's paper published in 1960,[92] in which he featured the utility of children as revealed in the demand for children, searching for both the price and income effects upon demand. Then, in 1965, came Becker's seminal presentation of a theory of the allocation of time. A useful, qualified summary of the core of the analytical problems in ascertaining the value that parents attribute to children is formulated by T. Paul Schultz as follows: [93]

[92] Gary S. Becker, "An Economic Analysis of Fertility," *Demographic and Economic Change in Developed Countries,* New York, NBER, 1960.

[93] T. Paul Schultz, "An Economic Model of Family Planning and Fertility," *Journal of Political Economy,* 77, March/April 1969, pp. 153–80.

The . . . problem is that of distinguishing between the demand for children and their supply, where parents are both the demanders and suppliers simultaneously. When one abstracts initially from the sources of uncertainty on the supply side, both from biological factors and the unreliability of birth control measures, the preferred reproductive behavior of parents is seen to depend on the following underlying values. With respect to the *demand* one has (1) the satisfactions of having a child (psychic utility that appears intangible because of the non-pecuniary context in which these satisfactions are obtained), and (2) the tangible returns that accrue to parents because of their child's future contribution to the parents' real income; with respect to *supply* one has (1) the opportunity and psychic costs of the parents' time and effort in bearing and rearing the child, and (2) the additional resource costs of rearing the child (tangible and as a rule pecuniary in nature). These distinctions may appear formal, arbitrary, and unhelpful to some, but they underscore the essential dual function of a child to his parents. The first category of determinants of both demand and supply is rooted in non-pecuniary values that resist tangible description and ordering, and are revealed only indirectly by means of micro analysis. . . . The second category of determinants is more likely to take a pecuniary form, submit to ordering, and admit to micro analysis.

Further advances in economic thinking with respect to fertility behavior appear in Robert J. Willis's Ph.D. dissertation, which has been in circulation among workers in this area for some time.[94] There have been supplementary studies by Mincer, Cain, Easterlin, and others.[95]

[94] Robert J. Willis, "The Economic Determinants of Fertility Behavior," Ph.D. dissertation, University of Washington, 1971; also, "A New Approach to the Economic Theory of Fertility Behavior," NBER, 1969 mimeo; and, jointly with Warren Sanderson, "Economic Models of Fertility: Some Examples and Implications," presented at the joint session of the American Economic Association and the American Statistical Association, Detroit, December 30, 1970.

[95] See Jacob Mincer, "The Labor Force Participation of Married Women," 1962; Glen G. Cain, *Married Women in the Labor Force,* 1966; and Richard A. Easterlin, *Population, Labor Force, and Long Swings in Economic Growth,* New York, Columbia University Press for NBER, 1968.

See also, among a long list of others:

Nathaniel H. Leff, "Dependency Rates and Savings Rates," *American Economic Review,* 59, December 1969, pp. 886–96; Paul Demeny, "Investment Allocation and Population Growth," *Demography,* 2, 1965, pp. 203–32; and Morris Silver, "Births, Marriages, and Business Cycles in the United States," *Journal of Political Economy,* 73, June 1965, pp. 237–55.

The research opportunities open to economists in the area of population have never been better than now. The demand for information about fertility, children, and population is strong both publicly and privately. The research possibilities have been advanced, especially by the extensions in economic theory concentrating on the behavior of parents in the household. A new economic perspective on population growth is emerging,[96] although a linkage between the new micro studies and macro analyses of population has not as yet been forged.

Economic explanations of completed fertility in widely different populations, using essentially the same theoretical approach, reveal comparable empirical results: Willis for the U.S. population, Michael for the U.S. suburban population, Gardner for U.S. farm women, Ben-Porath for Israel, and Schultz for Taiwan.[97] A critique of three of these studies by De Tray suggests that the theory is robust despite the limitations of the data and the overrefinement of some parts of the theory when it comes to empirical work.[98]

As noted earlier, the value of women's time is undoubtedly a key explanatory variable of fertility: Gronau's study is a basic approach in analyzing this variable; Michael's studies concentrate on the effects of education; and the value of woman's time and her education are strong in De Tray's study.[99]

[96] T. Paul Schultz, "An Economic Perspective on Population Growth," *Rapid Population Growth,* Vol. 2, Baltimore, Johns Hopkins Press, 1971.

[97] Robert J. Willis (see footnote 94); Robert T. Michael, "Education and Fertility," NBER, July 1971, unpublished; Bruce L. Gardner, "Economic Aspects of Rural-Farm Fertility in the United States," *Southern Economic Journal,* forthcoming; Yoram Ben-Porath, "Fertility in Israel, An Economist's Interpretation: Differentials and Trends, 1950–1970," Santa Monica, RAND, August 1970; "Fertility, Education and Income: A Different Context," paper presented at the Second World Congress of the Econometric Society, Cambridge, England, September 1970; and "Fertility, Education and Income in Cross Section Data in Israel," Jerusalem, Hebrew University, September 1971, unpublished; also, T. Paul Schultz, "Effectiveness of Family Planning in Taiwan: A Methodology for Program Evaluation," Santa Monica, RAND, July 1969.

[98] Dennis N. De Tray, "Substitution Between Quantity and Quality of Children in the Household," Ph.D. dissertation, University of Chicago, 1971.

[99] See Reuben Gronau, "The Intrafamily Allocation of Time and the Value of the Housewives' Time," Jerusalem, Hebrew University, June 1971, unpublished research report No. 28; Robert T. Michael, "Education and Fertility"; also, "The Effect of Education on Efficiency in Consumption," New York, NBER, forthcoming; Dennis N. De Tray (see footnote 98); and C. Russell Hill and Frank P. Stafford, "The Allocation of Time to Children and Educational Opportunities," University of Michigan, 1971, unpublished.

The behavioral pattern of marriage is also being investigated by economists. A theory of marriage has been advanced by Becker,[100] and empirical studies are in process by Freiden, Benham, and Reischaur.[101] Using mainly a transactions approach, Cheung has investigated marriage behavior in Chinese history.[102]

A modified theoretical approach to the economics of time and its application to consumer behavior is the burden of De Vany's Ph.D. research.[103] The demand for contraceptive information, goods, and services has been investigated by Cook.[104] Several additional studies that are under way using mainly the approach here under consideration are listed below.[105]

[100] Gary S. Becker, "A Theory of Marriage," workshop paper, University of Chicago, October 1971 (preceded by his "Notes on a Theory of Marriage," workshop paper, University of Chicago, October 1970).

[101] Alan Freiden, "An Econometric Model of Fertility, Labor Force Participation, and Migration," Ph.D. research in progress, University of Chicago, 1971; Lee Benham, "The Returns to Education of Women," workshop paper, University of Chicago, May 1971; Robert Reischaur, "Negro Family Relief and Marriage," Ph.D. research in progress, Columbia University, 1971.

[102] Steven N. S. Cheung, "Negative Dowry, Blind Marriage, and the Role of Ethics," unpublished paper, University of Washington, 1971.

[103] Arthur De Vany, "Time in the Budget of the Consumer: The Theory of Consumer Demand and Labor Supply Under a Time Constraint," Ph.D. dissertation, University of California, Los Angeles, 1970 (available as Professional Paper No. 36, Center for Naval Analyses, June 1970).

[104] William D. Cook, "Demand for Contraceptive Information, Goods and Services: An Analysis of the Orleans Parish Family Planning Program," Ph.D. dissertation, University of Chicago, 1971.

[105] Cynthia Brown, "Effects of Child Subsidy Programs on Fertility," unpublished paper, Barnard College, 1970; William P. Butz, "A Fertility Hypothesis Explaining the Long Period Decline of the U.S. Birth Rate," Ph.D. research in progress, University of Chicago, 1971; Alvin J. Harman, "Fertility and Economic Behavior of Families in the Philippines," Santa Monica, RAND, 1971, in progress; J. E. Koehler, "The Philippine Family Planning Program: Some Suggestions for Dealing with Uncertainties," Santa Monica, RAND, February 1970; Sue Ross, "The Spacing of Children," NBER, 1970, unpublished; Warren Sanderson, "Cohort Analysis to Determine the Probability of Birth," NBER, 1970, unpublished; T. Paul Schultz and Julie DaVanzo, "Analysis of Demographic Change in East Pakistan: A Study of Retrospective Survey Data," Santa Monica, RAND, 1971, in progress; James Smith, "Economic Analysis of Hours of Work," Ph.D. research in progress, University of Chicago, 1971; Larry J. Smith, "Income and Fertility: An Investment Approach," Ph.D. research in progress, University of Chicago, 1971; and Maurice Wilkinson, "Swedish and American Fertility Demand Functions," Ph. D. research in progress, Columbia University, 1971.

Alternative models to cope simultaneously with the effects on fertility of labor force participation, migration, death rates, education, marriage forms, location, contraceptive information, and income—using both space and time series data—have been advanced by Nerlove and Schultz.[106]

Although this list of policy issues is long, it is still incomplete. Among the omissions is the depressed areas problem, on which some fine work has been done by economists at North Carolina State University.[107] The poverty problem is also omitted, as well as the urban problem, both of which are in substantial part a consequence of particular lacks in human capital in the respective populations.

THE CHALLENGE OF ECONOMIC PUZZLES

As noted in section II, economists are often motivated in the research they undertake to find solutions to problems that have become known as puzzles. I shall begin with several general puzzles, the resolution of which appears to depend on the accounting of human capital, and then call attention to two that pertain to the agricultural sector, the sector that is best known to me. The residual, so it seems to me, is no longer a puzzle. A comment, however, is called for on what is lacking in the explanation of productivity change. With one exception,[108] to the best of my knowledge, there is no accounting of the differences in costs relative to returns between the different sources of the productivity change. But it is obvious that the improvements in the quality of material capital (forms) and in human capital (the acquired abilities of human agents) that explain a large part of the gains in productivity omitted in the empirical work that "produced" the residual have not been costless. But the solutions of the residual as they now stand, in general, conceal the relative rates of return to the investment that accounts for these quality components.

[106] Marc Nerlove and T. Paul Schultz, "Love and Life Between the Censuses: A Model of Family Decision Making in Puerto Rico, 1950–1960," Santa Monica, RAND, July 1970; and T. Paul Schultz, "A Framework for Analysis and Its Application to Taiwan's Family Planning Program," RAND, July 1971.

[107] Theodore W. Schultz, "Education and Economic Opportunities in Depressed Areas: Implications for Research," *Problems of Chronically Depressed Rural Areas,* Raleigh, North Carolina State University, 1965, pp. 45–53.

[108] The exception is the work of Zvi Griliches. See his paper "Notes on the Role of Education in Production Functions and Growth Accounting," in *Education, Income, and Human Capital,* W. Lee Hansen (ed.), New York, NBER 1970, pp. 71–115.

1. The Shrinkage of Capital Relative to Income in National Economic Accounting

The concepts of national income and capital and their measurement represent one of the major advances to come out of economics. The National Bureau of Economic Research has played a major role in contributing to this advance over the years. But it is increasingly clear that much remains to be done, and what needs doing is very much in the tradition of the kind of conceptual and measurement work at which the National Bureau excels. The unfinished work is revealed in the anomalies in national economic accounting that are not consistent with general economic thinking. In view of the abundance of capital that characterizes the U.S. economy and the increasing intensity in the use of capital that this accumulation of capital implies, it is hard to believe on economic grounds that the capital-income ratio should be declining and that the pace of capital formation in the United States should be slowing down. The source of these anomalies is that the concept of capital that enters in these national accounts omits much of the capital that is being accumulated, and that the estimates of saving that befit the partial concept of capital being used are way below the true savings that are actually taking place.

There are, as I have argued elsewhere, no compelling economic reasons why the stock of any particular class of capital should not fall (or rise) relative to national income over time.[109] Producer goods—structures, equipment, and inventories—are such a class. On the basis of my very crude estimates of human capital in the labor force, it would appear that the sum of the stock of this human capital and that of non-human capital relative to the net national product when expressed as a capital-income ratio was about 6, both in 1929 and 1957. Moreover, when human capital in the labor force is taken into account, the amount of capital formed may have been equal to about 26 per cent of the net national product for both years. While I have no intention of defending my estimates of the amount of human capital in the labor force, I do maintain that they suffice to suggest that *the omission of human capital in our national economic accounting seriously undermines the validity of these accounts*. With these remarks as a preface, I turn to the task of overhauling the gross national product.

[109] Theodore W. Schultz, "Reflections on Investment in Man," pp. 1–8.

2. The Growing Disbelief in GNP

GNP has become a popular symbol of what is wrong with the goals of economic policy. It is under attack from many quarters as a narrow, materialistic concept that is highly biased in favor of material affluence as a guide in evaluating production, consumption, and savings. There is some truth in these criticisms. The GNP is indeed only a partial concept in the way it is specified and estimated at present. A major overhauling is overdue, and a large part of what is missing in GNP consists in the components of human capital.

Meanwhile, endeavors to develop useful social goals for the purpose of determining national policy are reaching an impasse for lack of a meaningful common denominator for evaluating and rating the various social goals. Social theory provides no acceptable standard for determining the relative value to society of alternative social goals. The work by the panel and staff of the Department of Health, Education and Welfare that entered into the preparation of *Toward a Social Report* identifies a wide array of social goals: better health and less illness, opportunity for social mobility, improvement in the physical environment, reduction of poverty, less crime and more safety, advances in the sciences, arts, and learning, and still others.[110] But social theory and measurement do not suffice to rate the value of a given achievement with respect to any one of these social goals relative to that of the others. It is my contention that the extensions of economics as a consequence of the recent developments in economic theory and empirical analysis already referred to make it possible to bring some of these social goals into our national accounting and thus develop a more all-inclusive GNP.[111]

As argued above, the time has come for another major research

[110] Wilbur J. Cohen, *Toward a Social Report,* Washington, D.C., Department of Health, Education and Welfare, January 1969. This report is based on the extensive confidential study *Materials for a Preliminary Draft of the Social Report* by the Panel on Social Indicators, April 1968.

[111] John W. Kendrick is doing pioneer work in his recent studies in national income accounts. See his section in the *47th Annual Report,* NBER, June 1967, pp. 9–15, and "Restructuring the National Income Accounts for Investment and Growth Analysis," *Sartryck ur Statistisk Tidskrift,* 1966, 5. Also see Nancy Ruggles and Richard Ruggles, *The Design of Economic Accounts,* New York, National Bureau of Economic Research, 1970. Further, a large part of a recent paper by F. Thomas Juster is a clear and cogent analysis of this issue; see his "New Directions on National Bureau Research," presented at a joint session of the American Economic Association and the American Statistical Association, Detroit, December 30, 1970.

endeavor to extend the concepts of the components of GNP. It requires the Kuznets genius in developing concepts and in devising measurement within a research organization that can and will support the slow, painstaking task of producing the necessary data, at least up to the point where it is clear that such data can be had and the public agencies are prepared to take over and continue the task.

A beginning effort in what is required is already at hand. It is no surprise that it should have come from Kuznets. Building on my estimates that show that the outlay on formal education in 1956 in the United States was $28.7 billion, of which $12.4 billion was income foregone, Kuznets presents the following analysis: [112]

> If we omit the [income foregone], the residual $16.3 billion can be compared with a total gross material capital formation for that year of $79.5 billion. . . . If direct costs of formal education alone are over 20 per cent of gross capital formation, outlays on education, health, and recreation, treatable as investment in man, may well be as high as four tenths of capital formation. If so, the distribution of gross national product, net of intermediate products, would be not 70 per cent for consumption and 30 per cent for capital formation, but perhaps 58 per cent and 42 per cent, respectively.
>
> Further adjustments in the magnitude of total product and in its allocation between consumption and capital formation will occur when we take account of costs of income foregone, and, more generally, of the uses of time not committed to gainful work (or so committed at lower-than-possible compensation for the sake of learning). Two approaches can be followed. First, we can merely add the cost of income foregone in formal education and in on-the-job training to both countrywide product and educational investment in man. In 1957, investment in formal education net of income foregone and investment in on-the-job training of males in the labor force, all of which is income foregone, were about the same, $18.2 and $18.6 billion, respectively.[113] . . . If, then, we add 10 per cent to "pure" GNP and to the capital formation component, the dis-

[112] Simon Kuznets, *Modern Economic Growth,* New Haven, Yale University Press, 1966, pp. 228–33.

[113] Using my estimates, Kuznets set the proportion of income foregone to total outlays on formal education at 40 per cent, and, by applying this proportion to the increment to educational capital in the population, obtained $18.2 billion for investment in education in 1957, net of income foregone.

tribution between total consumption and capital formation, put at 58 and 42 per cent, respectively, at the end of the preceding paragraph, now becomes 53 per cent for consumption and 47 per cent for capital formation.

The second approach requires the addition of the value of all time released by the reduction in working hours accompanying economic growth, and of the income foregone in on-the-job training, to countrywide product and to the relevant components. The full value of released time should be included because this released time is a major result of economic growth and because much of the allocation of consumption, and even the use of the time for further education, is not comprehensible unless some magnitude is assigned to the increased leisure. A rough calculation for the United States, which sets the value of an hour released from work at the average labor product per work hour in the economy, yields a magnitude for 1939–48 that is as much as 40 per cent of GNP.[114] If we assume the same proportional magnitude to "pure" GNP (i.e., excluding intermediate products in government and private consumption) and add 6 per cent for income foregone in on-the-job training, the revised countrywide product total becomes 146—of which consumption, including leisure, accounts for 58 points (as indicated above) plus 40 points for total leisure minus 4 points representing time spent and income foregone in formal education, or a total of 94 points; whereas capital formation, which amounted to 42 points, is augmented by the 10 points allowed for income foregone in formal education and on-the-job training—and the final allocation is 64 per cent for total consumption including leisure and 36 per cent for total capital formation including costs of income foregone. . . .

Kuznets then makes the point that these extensions of GNP are an effort to take account of fundamental issues in the analysis of economic growth. He concludes with these observations:

First, despite the crudity of the assumptions and of the resulting estimates, the main points in the analysis should be clear. Given the close association between the structural changes accompanying economic growth on the production side and the many components

[114] Simon Kuznets, "Long-Term Changes," in *Income and Wealth of the United States,* Series II, Cambridge, Bowes and Bowes, 1952, Tables 1 and 7, pp. 30 and 65.

of consumption required (either as extra costs or as extra investment in human beings) to assure effective participation of people in
the productive process, the presently accepted national accounting
definitions of the net totals and the distinctions between consumption and capital formation leave much to be desired. The accepted
definitions and distinctions are based upon the purpose for which
a good is purchased and on the status of the purchaser as an "enterprise"—a unit bent largely on profit. If a good is *not* purchased for
resale (with or without some transformation), it is defined as a
"final" product, even if it is used by the purchaser (household or
government) to cover costs connected with the operation of the
economy, or as investment in education. If a good is purchased by
an enterprise but has a long life and is not intended for *immediate*
resale, then it is a final capital good. But the resale principle, while
suitable for the analysis of short-term changes with particular emphasis on possible shortages or excesses of purchasing power, is
hardly a useful criterion in the analysis of long-term trends and
structural changes involved in economic growth. The connection
between the use of a good and its effect on long-term trends in output and efficiency is poorly defined by resale; and in view of the
importance of quality of human beings as a factor in economic
growth, total consumption as now defined cannot be considered
completely free of elements of investment in human beings, or of
elements of additional costs imposed upon people by the changing
conditions of participation in economic production.

Second, if investment in human beings and foregone income
are recognized, the whole pattern of use of time—in addition to the
use of goods—must be considered. For, after all, time at the disposal
of human beings is a basic and limited resource. It must therefore
be explicitly understood that the release of more time from engagement in direct production of commodities and services is an important aspect of economic growth, an important part of its total
product; and regardless of the difficulties involved, it must be given
an explicit weight. Consequently, we cannot limit measurement to
what has actually been produced but must attempt to estimate what
might have been produced if the drain upon a basic limited resource
had remained unchanged.

Third, to return to the problems of distinction and estimation,
calculations like those summarized [here] are obviously crude

guesses, whose primary value lies largely in indicating minimal orders of magnitude. More useful measures would require an intensive analysis of consumption, capital formation, and time use by the human beings who comprise the economic society. In the process, such difficult problems as distinguishing between education as investment and education as consumption, or between consumption demanded by a job and consumption to satisfy personal needs, would have to be faced and satisfactory operating and empirically testable answers sought for. Furthermore, the definition and valuation of time released from direct engagement in producing commodities and services would have to be sharpened and tested.

What is presently possible in extending the concept of GNP using the work pertaining to human capital cannot be taken beyond the perceptive thinking of Kuznets. The new economic theorizing with respect to crime and punishment, accidents, discrimination, and other areas still awaits empirical application in ways that may provide results that could be made an integral part of GNP. Nor are the losses from pollution taken into account.

3. The Leontief Paradox

This paradox, along with the increasing awareness of the seminal economic properties of human capital, has led to a good deal of fruitful research in the area of international trade. A recent paper by Kenen brings us up to date on the findings pertaining to the role of human capital in determining the comparative advantage of nations.[115] There is no need to summarize Kenen's paper, for it is readily available in the economic literature sponsored by the National Bureau. There is, however, a closely related issue that calls for research on which I wish to dwell briefly. In an endeavor to explain the differences in per capita income among nations, Krueger, in her pioneering paper on factor endowments and per capita income, concludes "that the difference in human resources between the United States and the less-developed countries accounts for more of the differences in *per capita* income than all the other factors combined." [116] In view of the radical implications of her findings for eco-

[115] Peter B. Kenen, "Skills, Human Capital, and Comparative Advantage," in *Education, Income, and Human Capital,* W. Lee Hansen (ed.), New York, NBER, 1970, pp. 195–230.

[116] Anne O. Krueger, "Factor Endowments and *Per Capita* Income Differences among Countries," *Economic Journal,* 78, September 1968, pp. 641–59.

nomic development, what is called for is a critical analysis of her method, data, and inferences, and an effort to duplicate the research and thus either confirm her conclusion or show that it lacks validity.

4. Accounting for the Tendency Toward More Equality in the Distribution of Personal Income under Modern Capitalism [117]

This tendency has become a well-established fact, but explanations of this phenomenon are still in their infancy. Progressive taxation is only a part of the explanation. The modest decline in the inequality of the distribution of personal wealth explains very little. The part that income transfers play via public expenditures on welfare programs other than on schooling is probably small, measured in terms of their progressive effects on the distribution of personal income. The equity effects of schooling and higher education on this tendency, already noted, are important. In reaching for a more general explanation, I would favor the following hypothesis: *The increases in the demand for skills and knowledge and the response of the supply that is under way in modern economies lead to the accumulation of forms of human capital that accounts for most of the observed tendency under consideration.*

5. The Farm Income–Farm Wealth Puzzle

Poverty among farm families in the United States is relatively high despite the fact that the sector's personal wealth is high.[118] The Economic Report of the President of January 1964 classifies families with incomes less than $3,000 as falling below the poverty line. It shows, using 1962 data, that 18 per cent of the nonfarm and 43 per cent of the farm families were below this line at that time.[119] Thus, by this measure, the relative poverty was two and one-half times as high among farm as among nonfarm families. The data on wealth appear to tell a wholly different story, according to the survey reported in the Federal Reserve Bulletin of March 1964. It shows that the net worth per farm family was twice as large as that of the population as a whole. The per family figures that follow are the mean amounts as of December 1962 (the medians are also shown for the totals).

[117] See references listed in footnotes 30 and 31.
[118] Theodore W. Schultz, *Economic Growth and Agriculture,* New York, McGraw-Hill, 1968, pp. 237–38.
[119] Half of this farm poverty was in the South, according to the 1960 Census.

	All U.S. Families	Farm Operator Families
Own home	$ 5,975	$ 5,501
Automobile	637	681
Business, professions	3,913	25,767
Life insurance, annuities, retirement plans	1,376	1,278
Liquid assets	2,579	2,309
Stocks	4,072	1,354
Bonds	456	535
Other	2,535	5,940
Miscellaneous	1,528	1,095
Personal debt (excluding automobile)	483	486
Total net worth		
(1) Mean	$22,588	$43,973
(2) Median	7,550	26,250

Granted that these two sets of data are not comparable in several respects, when account is taken of supporting evidence the general implications are nevertheless probably valid, and thus the farm income and the farm wealth differences are puzzling. The resolution of this puzzle appears to depend in part on what has been happening to earnings relative to the income from property in U.S. agriculture. The earnings from farm work have long been depressed, as is obvious from the migration out of agriculture. The income from farm land has been increasing due in no small part to federal subsidies and associated effects of the agricultural programs. Thus, the aggregate earnings from human capital in agriculture have been depressed, while the income from farm property (land) has been subsidized, with strong regressive effects on the distribution of personal income within agriculture.[120]

6. The Failure of Migration and Schooling as Solutions to Farm Poverty

A widely held tenet in economics has been that high employment, movement of people leaving the depressed sector, and schooling are of

[120] An explanation of the income inequalities within agriculture appears in the first four chapters of the study by Bruce L. Gardner "An Analysis of U.S. Farm Family Income Inequality, 1950–1960," Ph.D. dissertation, University of Chicago, 1968.

critical importance in reducing sectoral poverty, whether it be in agriculture, coal mining, or in the textile industry. I, too, have long held to this tenet, but the puzzle arises out of results from a careful empirical analysis of changes in agriculture during recent years, and they do not provide support for this tenet. Gardner's study of farm family income inequalities suggests that neither schooling nor migration has proved to be a solution.[121] The reason appears to be the inability of poor farm people to respond adequately to shifts in the demand for skills by migrating or by acquiring additional skills. The explanation is to be found, so it appears, in capital rationing as it influences the acquisition of human capital under these circumstances.

ADVANCES IN THE TECHNOLOGY OF ECONOMICS

The research opportunities are now neatly arranged in two lots. One is large with many different policy issues on display, and the other contains a few puzzles. In deciding how much to pay for any of these offerings, it is the better part of wisdom to make sure that the economist who would be saddled with it is equipped to do it. Obsolescence has not been gentle in its treatment of economists, as is clear from the recent changes in the state of economics. Work in the area of human capital calls for new approaches made possible by particular advances in the technology of economics. Some of these advances have already been considered, mainly in connection with the various classes of policy issues. What remains to be done, therefore, is to consider some of the additional properties of these advances in analyzing the role of human capital in the economic system and to present some of the hypotheses that have emerged.

1. The production function is now widely used in econometrics. But what can it tell us about human capital? Except for education, it remains to be seen what the results will be. In the case of education, however, Griliches has shown that education as a variable in aggregate production functions is significant and is well-behaved.[122] If, however, one doubts the earnings functions and the rates of return attributed to education, can this technique provide independent answers to the following questions: Does education really increase productivity? Is the contribution of education, as it is measured by the other methods that are being

[121] Ibid., Chapter 5.
[122] Zvi Griliches, "Notes on the Role of Education in Production Functions and Growth Accounting," 1970.

used, approximately correct? In nailing down these doubts, Griliches
has examined the role of the education variable by means of econometric aggregate production function studies. The answers that emerge
are in the affirmative.

2. The application of the production function technique in analyzing the economic efficiency of schools and universities as producers of
educational services, has, to the best of my knowledge, not been successful as yet.[123]

3. The technique of Distributed Lags has been widely used in
economics following the classic contributions of Nerlove in developing
this technique.[124] Despite the empirical usefulness of this technique, there
has been a surprising lack of attempts to bring economic theory to bear
in specifying the lags that would be acceptable on economic grounds.[125]
A notable exception is the approach that Welch used in formulating the
hypothesis that the length of the lags of farmers as entrepreneurs in
decoding information about new inputs, in adopting them, and in using
them efficiently depends upon the level of their schooling, and that the
higher the level of schooling, the shorter the lag.[126] The economic reasons
for this pattern of lags are cogent and the empirical analysis supports the
economic theory from which the hypothesis is derived.[127] In view of the
sources of the dynamics of the economy, in substantial part from streams
of new and better inputs, the Welch hypothesis should be further tested
to see whether the effects of education on entrepreneurial abilities in
other sectors support the hypothesis.

4. It could be that the missing link between functional and personal
income has been discovered. It appears to be human capital earnings in
labor income. The recent survey by Mincer supports this inference, as

[123] Samuel Bowles's perceptive paper "Towards an Educational Production
Function," in *Education, Income, and Human Capital,* points out the many difficult,
unsolved problems. These difficulties also were stressed by Henry Levin in his
recent workshop presentation at the University of Chicago.

[124] Marc Nerlove, *The Dynamics of Supply: Estimation of Farmers' Response
to Price,* Baltimore, Johns Hopkins Press, 1958. For a comprehensive survey, see
Zvi Griliches, "Distributed Lags: A Survey," *Econometrica,* 35, July 1967, pp.
16–49.

[125] This issue is the central thrust of Nerlove's Henry Schultz Memorial
Lecture "On Lags in Economic Behavior" before the Econometric Society's
meeting in Cambridge on September 8, 1970.

[126] Finis Welch, "Education in Production," 1970.

[127] Support for this hypothesis also appears in the study by D. P. Chaudhri
"Farmers' Education and Productivity: Some Empirical Results from Indian
Agriculture," Human Capital Paper No. 69:04, University of Chicago, 1969.

already noted.[128] Viewed as a hypothesis awaiting further testing, it holds that a General Earnings Function that accounts for all of the human capital components, i.e., the earnings from schooling and higher education, postschool and also preschool attainments, and from the other forms of human capital will explain most of the distribution of personal income and the changes occurring in it over time under recent and existing circumstances in the United States.

5. The economic reasoning underlying the distinction between *general* and *specific* human capital, developed by Becker with special reference to on-the-job training, is strong and clear.[129] But it is odd that work on specific human capital should have been so neglected, except for the very recent studies by Telser and then Parsons, following up Telser's approach.[130] The Telser hypothesis is that specific human capital is one of the determinants of the rates of return in manufacturing, and his test supports the hypothesis.

6. It is formally correct to think of the stock of human capital as the sum of two components: innate ability and acquired ability. The economics of innate ability is closely akin to that of the original properties of land underlying Ricardian rent. The assumptions that the level and distribution of innate abilities in large populations are approximately the same and that in any time span that is relevant in economic analysis the innate ability of these populations cannot be altered appreciably are probably valid. But what remains unknown, despite a large literature, is the economic value of this ability and the role it plays in human capital. It is obviously a major issue that should be faced and settled, assuming that it is possible to do so.

It is not uncommon in confronting a basic issue not to ask the right question in seeking a solution. With respect to education under existing circumstances, given the underlying supply of and demand for innate ability, it is increasingly doubtful that a significant part of the earnings attributed to schooling and even to higher education is an *economic rent* to innate ability. The attempts that have been made to adjust the additional earnings associated with additional education may be unwarranted

[128] Jacob Mincer, "The Distribution of Labor Incomes," 1970.

[129] Gary S. Becker, "Investment in Human Capital: A Theoretical Analysis," *Journal of Political Economy,* 70, supplement, October 1962, pp. 9–49.

[130] Lester Telser, "Some Determinants of the Rates of Return in Manufacturing," University of Chicago, 1968, unpublished paper, and "An Analysis of Turnover in Selected Manufacturing Industries," University of Chicago, 1969, unpublished paper; see also Donald O. Parsons, "Specific Human Capital: Layoffs and Quits," Ph.D. dissertation, University of Chicago, 1970.

in view of the supply-demand characteristics of innate ability and its dependency on investment, for it, too, acquires some economic value. In formulating the hypothesis that follows I have been influenced by the perceptive treatment of "ability" by Griliches.[131]

By way of preface to the hypothesis, it assumes that the classification of people made in accordance with their innate abilities consists of classes that are sufficiently broad to encompass a large number of people. Thus, it is not a classification that is so fine that it identifies the ten best movie stars or the ten best baseball players. Instead, it is a classification of students into four or five classes on the basis of their presumed IQs.

The innate ability hypothesis here advanced is as follows: When the innate ability of a large population is classified into four or five classes, the "original" supply of innate ability in each class, under existing demand conditions, is such that at the relevant margins there is only a small significant economic rent to innate ability, and that the investment made to develop the innate ability of each class accounts for most of the value added, albeit the difference in the amounts invested depends on the differences in innate ability. In other words, each class of innate ability is still an "abundant" resource in a population as large as that of the United States, and therefore innate ability per se, considering its supply and the demand for it in the population and the economy as a whole, has only a small economic value.

An analogy based on rent to land may be helpful at this point. Suppose we start with no-rent dry land in California and Montana. Assume that a part of this dry land is then improved by means of investment in irrigation (with a part, however, remaining unused as no-rent land). The productive capacity of improved land in California can be enhanced much more than in Montana for reasons of the difference in climate. In either case, however, the difference between the two locations that is arrived at is a function of the difference in the amounts invested. The observed difference in "rent" to the improved parts would be predominantly a return to the difference in the investment made. This analogy

[131] See section 5 of the paper by Zvi Griliches "Notes on the Role of Education in Production Functions and Growth Accounting," 1970. In addition, two new papers are now at hand on this issue. They show that innate ability measured by standard IQ tests account for a small part of the observed differences in earnings. See Zvi Griliches, "Education, Income, and Ability," and John C. Hause, "Ability and Schooling as Determinants of Lifetime Earnings," presented at COBRE Workshop on Higher Education, Equity and Efficiency, June 7–10, 1971, to be published in *Journal of Political Economy* in 1972.

can be generalized and applied to innate ability on the assumption, set forth in the preface, that when the innate abilities are classified into relatively few classes, each consisting of a large number of persons, the supply of each such class of innate ability under existing demand conditions is virtually a "free resource." Thus, to repeat, at the margin there is little economic rent for it. Accordingly, what we observe for each class is the return to investment in human capital starting from the margin of a small rent for innate ability. In short, *this hypothesis states that in a population of over 200 million people the supply of the higher levels of innate ability is sufficiently large to keep its economic value small.*

7. The extension of economic theory to deal with the effects of discrimination upon the formation and utilization of human capital is proving to be increasingly useful. Both in terms of theory and empirical analysis, the new thrust began with Becker's book (first edition, 1957).[132] Welch has used it with modifications; his results have already been cited under policy issues pertaining to schooling.[133] Becker's preface to the new edition of his book reviews the main issues that have arisen in the use of this analytical tool since the publication of the 1957 edition.

8. Bowles [134] has shown that a planning model with special reference to education produces meaningful empirical results. There is a large family of planning models attempting to integrate manpower planning and educational planning, including some linear programming models.[135] The critical appraisal of these models by Bowman points up the analytical difficulties, and particularly the lack of data to implement such models.[136] Bowles's empirical analysis using his model is modest in that it is restricted to the educational sector of Northern Nigeria (also to Greece), treating the educational inputs and the demand for the skills acquired by means of education as exogenously determined. His results are readily transformed into rates of return for each of the subsectors of

[132] Gary S. Becker, *The Economics of Discrimination*, 1971.

[133] Finis Welch, "Labor Market Discrimination," 1967.

[134] Samuel Bowles, "Efficiency in the Allocation of Resources to Education: A Planning Model with Application to Northern Nigeria," Ph.D. dissertation, Harvard University, 1965. Bowles has also applied this model to Greece.

[135] Samuel Bowles, *Planning Educational Systems for Economic Growth*, Cambridge, Harvard University Press, 1969, is an excellent presentation of the planning problem in education and review of various classes of models that have been developed for this purpose.

[136] Mary Jean Bowman, "The Human Investment Revolution in Economic Thought," 1966. The planning approach is also discussed by C. Arnold Anderson and Mary Jean Bowman, "Theoretical Considerations in Education Planning," in *Educational Planning*, Don Adams (ed.), Syracuse, Syracuse University Press, 1965.

the educational system. What is lacking here and also in the rate-of-return studies is an explanation of the changes in the demand for each of the different levels of skills associated with schooling and higher education.

9. The logical basis for the concept of earnings foregone, the empirical possibilities of estimating them, the importance of earnings foregone as an opportunity cost in on-the-job training and in attending high school and college, and the wide array of puzzles related to the incentives to invest in human capital for which earnings foregone offer a consistent and unified explanation are well-established.[137] Nonetheless, Vaizey [138] and associates continue to protest the usefulness of this concept, despite the sharp criticism by Johnson of Vaizey's reasoning and the extended treatment of the costing of the development of human resources by Bowman.[139] The changing pattern of earnings foregone in the United States has made earlier estimates obsolete; [140] clearly, new empirical work is called for.

10. The allocation of one's own time (earnings foregone) in acquiring human capital led Becker to treat the value of time as a fundamental cost component in individual allocative decisions, both in consumption and in participating in the labor force. His classic paper "A Theory of the Allocation of Time" is rapidly proving to be a seminal extension of economic theory.[141] Professor Johnson states it succinctly, as already noted: "The central principle of the analysis is that in reality each consumer good has two prices attached to it—a money price, as in the traditional theory of consumer choice, and a time cost of acquiring and consuming the commodity. The money price is, however, resolvable into the worktime required to earn it, so that consumption and labor-supply decisions are both facets of the allocation of time, the individual's basic resource." [142]

[137] Theodore W. Schultz, *The Economic Value of Education,* New York, Columbia University Press, 1963, pp. 27–32.

[138] Manuela F. Leite, Patrick Lynch, John Sheehan, and John Vaizey, *The Economics of Educational Costing,* Parts I and III A, Centro de Economica e Finanças, Lisbon, 1968 and 1969.

[139] Harry G. Johnson, "A Comment," *The Residual Factor and Economic Growth,* Paris, OECD, 1964, pp. 225–27; and Mary Jean Bowman, "The Costing of Human Resource Development," E. A. G. Robinson and John E. Vaizey (eds.), *The Economics of Education,* New York, St. Martin's Press, 1966, pp. 421–50.

[140] Theodore W. Schultz, *Investment in Human Capital,* 1971, Chapter 7.

[141] Gary S. Becker, "A Theory of the Allocation of Time," 1965.

[142] Harry G. Johnson, "The Economic Approach to Social Questions," 1968, pp. 8–9.

The value of the time of members of the household, as an economic variable, has added an important new dimension to the theory of the household. Papers that are as yet unpublished by Becker and empirical studies guided by this development attest to the significance of this advance in economics.[143]

11. The extension of traditional economic theory to cope with investment in human capital is now well known and widely used. Although it is basic in pursuing many of the research opportunities that have been identified in this paper, it is already part and parcel of the literature of the National Bureau and thus requires no elaboration here.

It is time, however, for the visible hand of supply and demand to take over, not only to add to and subtract from what has been presented but more importantly, to rate and assign priorities to the research opportunities in human capital relative to all alternative research opportunities.

SELECTED BIBLIOGRAPHY

The following list includes books, journal papers, and unpublished manuscripts referred to in the text, as well as additional selected items from the many now available, both published and in manuscript form. To supplement this listing, the reader will find the following publications helpful: Mark Blaug, *Economics of Education: A Selected Annotated Bibliography,* 2nd ed., London, Pergamon Press, 1971; W. Lee Hansen (ed.), *Education, Income, and Human Capital,* Studies in Income and Wealth, Vol. 35, New York, NBER, 1970; Theodore W. Schultz, *The Economic Value of Education,* New York, Columbia University Press, 1963; and Theodore W. Schultz (ed.), "Investment in Education: The Equity-Efficiency Quandary," *Journal of Political Economy,* 80, supplement, May/June 1972, forthcoming.

[143] Gary S. Becker, "The Allocation of Time and Goods over Time," June 1967, unpublished paper; "Consumption Theory: Some Criticisms and a Suggested Approach," May 1968, unpublished paper; "A Theory of Social Interactions," September 1969, unpublished paper (a revision and substantial modification of his "Interdependent Preferences: Charity, Externalities, and Income Taxation," March 1968, unpublished); also, Robert T. Michael, "Effects of Education," NBER, forthcoming; Michael Grossman, "The Demand for Health," Ph.D. dissertation, Columbia University, 1969; Gilbert Ghez, "A Model of Life Cycle Consumption Behavior and the Allocation of Time," Ph.D. dissertation, Columbia University, 1970.

Closely related are: Yoram Ben-Porath, "The Production of Human Capital and the Life Cycle of Earnings," 1967, and "The Production of Human Capital Over Time," in *Education, Income, and Human Capital,* New York, NBER, 1970; Kelvin J. Lancaster, "A New Approach to Consumer Theory," *Journal of Political Economy,* 74, April 1966, pp. 132–57.

Abramovitz, Moses. *Resources and Output Trends in the United States Since 1870.* Occasional Paper 52. New York: NBER, 1956.

Alchian, Armen. "Uncertainty, Evolution, and Economic Theory." *Journal of Political Economy* 58 (June 1950): 211–21.

Anderson, C. Arnold, and Bowman, Mary Jean. "Theoretical Considerations in Educational Planning." In *Educational Planning,* Don Adams (ed.). Syracuse: Syracuse University Press, 1965.

Archibald, George C. "Chamberlin Versus Chicago." *Review of Economic Studies* 29 (October 1961): 1–28.

Becker, Gary S. "An Economic Analysis of Fertility." In *Demographic and Economic Change in Developed Countries.* Universities–National Bureau Conference Series II. New York: NBER, 1960.

———. "Irrational Behavior and Economic Theory." *Journal of Political Economy* 70 (February 1962): 1–13.

———. "Investment in Human Capital: A Theoretical Analysis." *Journal of Political Economy* 70 (October 1962, supplement): 9–49.

———. *Human Capital: A Theoretical and Empirical Analysis, with Special Reference to Education.* New York: NBER, 1964.

———. "A Theory of the Allocation of Time." *Economic Journal* 75 (September 1965): 493–517.

———. "The Allocation of Time and Goods over Time." Unpublished paper, NBER, June 1967.

———. *Human Capital and the Personal Distribution of Income: An Analytical Approach.* Woytinsky Lecture No. 1, Institute of Public Administration, University of Michigan, 1967.

———. "Consumption Theory: Some Criticisms and a Suggested Approach." Unpublished paper, Columbia University, May 1968.

———. "A Theory of Social Interactions." Unpublished paper, University of Chicago, September 1969. (Substantial revision of "Interdependent Preferences: Charity, Externalities, and Income Taxation," unpublished paper, March 1968.)

———. "Notes on a Theory of Marriage." Workshop paper, University of Chicago, October 1970.

———. *Economic Theory.* New York: Alfred A. Knopf, 1971.

———. *The Economics of Discrimination.* 2nd ed. Chicago: University of Chicago Press, 1971.

———. "A Theory of Marriage." Workshop paper, University of Chicago, October 1971.

Becker, Gary S., and Chiswick, Barry R. "Education and the Distribution of Earnings." *American Economic Review* 56 (May 1966): 358–69.

Benham, Lee. "The Returns to Education of Women." Workshop paper, University of Chicago, May 1971.

Ben-Porath, Yoram. "Some Aspects of the Life Cycle of Earnings." Ph.D. dissertation, Harvard University, 1967.

———. "The Production of Human Capital and the Life Cycle of Earnings." *Journal of Political Economy* 75 (August 1967): 352–65.

———. "Fertility in Israel, An Economist's Interpretation: Differentials and Trends, 1950–1970." Santa Monica: RAND, August 1970.

———. "The Production of Human Capital over Time." In *Education, Income, and*

Human Capital, W. Lee Hansen (ed.), Studies in Income and Wealth, Vol. 35, pp. 129–47. New York: NBER, 1970.

————. "Fertility, Education and Income: A Different Context." Paper presented at the Second World Congress of the Econometric Society, Cambridge, England, September 1970.

————. "The Association between Fertility and Education." Research report 20, Department of Economics, Hebrew University, Jerusalem, 1971.

————. "Fertility, Education and Income in Cross Section Data in Israel." Unpublished paper, Hebrew University, Jerusalem, September 1971.

Bowles, Samuel. "The Efficient Allocation of Resources to Education: A Planning Model with Application to Northern Nigeria." Ph.D. dissertation, Harvard University, 1965.

————. *Planning Educational Systems for Economic Growth.* Cambridge: Harvard University Press, 1969.

————. "Towards an Educational Production Function." In *Education, Income, and Human Capital,* W. Lee Hansen (ed.), Studies in Income and Wealth, Vol. 35, pp. 11–61. New York: NBER, 1970.

Bowman, Mary Jean. "The Costing of Human Resource Development." In *The Economics of Education,* E. A. G. Robinson and John E. Vaizey (eds.), pp. 421–50. New York: St. Martin's Press, 1966.

————. "The Human Investment Revolution in Economic Thought." *Sociology of Education* 39 (Spring 1966): 111–37.

————. "Principles in the Valuation of Human Capital." *Review of Income and Wealth,* Series 14 (September 1968): 217–46.

Bowman, Mary Jean, and Anderson, C. Arnold. "Distributional Effects of Educational Programs." In *Income Distribution Analysis,* Series 23. Raleigh: North Carolina State University, 1966.

Bowman, Mary Jean, and Myers, Robert G. "Schooling, Experience and Gains and Losses in Human Capital Through Migration." *Journal of the American Statistical Association* 62 (September 1967): 875–98.

Brown, Cynthia. "Effects of Child Subsidy Programs on Fertility." Unpublished paper, Barnard College, 1970.

Butz, William P. "A Fertility Hypothesis Explaining the Long Period Decline of the U.S. Birth Rate." Ph.D. research in progress, University of Chicago, 1971.

Cain, Glen G. *Married Women in the Labor Force.* Chicago: University of Chicago Press, 1966.

————. "Issues in the Economics of a Population Policy for the United States." *American Economic Review* 61 (May 1971): 408–17.

Cain, Glen G., and Weininger, Adriana. "Economic Determinants of Fertility." Unpublished paper, University of Wisconsin, 1971.

Carnegie Commission on Higher Education. *Quality and Equality: Revised Recommendations, New Levels of Federal Responsibility for Higher Education.* New York: McGraw-Hill, 1970.

Chaudhri, D. P. "Education and Agricultural Productivity in India." Ph.D. dissertation, University of Delhi, 1968.

————. "Farmers' Education and Productivity: Some Empirical Results from Indian Agriculture." Human Capital Paper 69:04, University of Chicago, 1969.

Cheung, Steven N. S. "Negative Dowry, Blind Marriage, and the Role of Ethics." Unpublished paper, University of Washington, 1971.

Chiswick, Barry R. "Human Capital and the Distribution of Personal Income by Regions." Ph.D. dissertation, Columbia University, 1967.

―――. "The Average Level of Schooling and the Personal Distribution of Income by Regions: A Clarification." *American Economic Review* 58 (June 1968): 495–500.

―――. "Earnings Inequality and Economic Development." *Quarterly Journal of Economics* 85 (February 1971): 21–39.

Cohen, Wilbur J. *Toward a Social Report*. Washington, D.C.: U.S. Department of Health, Education, and Welfare, January 1969.

Cohn, Elchanan; Gifford, Adam; and Sharkansky, Ira. "Comments." *Journal of Human Resources* 5 (Spring 1970): 222–36.

Coleman, James. "The Concept of Equality of Educational Opportunity." In "Equal Educational Opportunity," special issue, *Harvard Educational Review* 38 (Winter 1968): 7–22.

Coleman, James S. et al. *Equality of Educational Opportunity*. 2 vols. Washington, D.C.: U.S. Government Printing Office, 1966.

Conrad, A. R., and Meyer, J. R. "The Economics of Slavery in the Antebellum South." *Journal of Political Economy* 66 (April 1958): 95–130.

Cook, William D. "Demand for Contraceptive Information, Goods and Services: An Analysis of the Orleans Parish Family Planning Program." Ph.D. dissertation, University of Chicago, 1971.

Demeny, Paul. "Investment Allocation and Population Growth." *Demography* 2 (1965): 203–32.

Demsetz, Harold. "Minorities in the Market Place." *North Carolina Law Review* 43 (February 1965): 272–97.

Denison, Edward F. *The Sources of Economic Growth in the United States and the Alternatives Before Us*. Supplementary paper 13. New York: Committee for Economic Development, 1962.

―――. "Measuring the Contribution of Education." In *The Residual Factor and Economic Growth*, pp. 13–55 and 77–102. Paris: OECD, 1964.

―――. "An Aspect of the Inequality of Opportunity." *Journal of Political Economy* 78 (September/October 1970): 1195–1202.

De Tray, Dennis N. "Substitution between Quantity and Quality of Children in the Household." Ph.D. dissertation, University of Chicago, 1971.

De Vany, Arthur. "Time in the Budget of Consumers: The Theory of Consumer Demand and Labor Supply Under a Time Constraint." Ph.D. dissertation, University of California, Los Angeles, 1970. (Listed as professional paper 36, Center for Naval Analyses, June 1970.)

Dugan, D. J. "The Impact of Parental and Educational Investment upon School Achievement." *Proceedings of the Social Statistics Section, American Statistical Association*, 1969.

Easterlin, Richard A. *Population, Labor Force, and Long Swings in Economic Growth*. New York: NBER, 1968.

―――. "Does Human Fertility Adjust to the Environment?" *American Economic Review* 61 (May 1971): 399–407.

Fisher, Irving. "What Is Capital?" *Economic Journal* 6 (December 1896): 509–34.

————. "Senses of Capital." *Economic Journal* 7 (June 1897): 199–213.

————. "Precedents for Defining Capital." *Quarterly Journal of Economics* 18 (March 1904): 386–408.

————. *The Nature of Capital and Income*. New York and London: Macmillan Company, 1906.

Fishlow, Albert. "Levels of Nineteenth Century American Investment in Education." *Journal of Economic History* 26 (December 1966): 418–36.

Freeman, Richard B. "Discrimination against College-Educated Blacks." Economics workshop paper, University of Chicago, February 1971.

————. *The Market for College-Trained Manpower: A Study in the Economics of Career Choice*. Cambridge: Harvard University Press, 1971.

————. *Black Elite*. New York: McGraw-Hill, forthcoming.

Freiden, Alan. "An Econometric Model of Fertility, Labor Force Participation, and Migration." Ph.D. research in progress, University of Chicago, 1971.

Friedman, Milton. "The Methodology of Positive Economics." In *Essays in Positive Economics,* pp. 3–43. Chicago: University of Chicago Press, 1953.

————. *A Theory of the Consumption Function*. Princeton: Princeton University Press for NBER, 1957.

Friedman, Milton, and Kuznets, Simon. *Income from Independent Professional Practice*. New York: NBER, 1945.

Gardner, Bruce L. "An Analysis of U.S. Farm Family Income Inequality, 1950–1960." Ph. D. dissertation, University of Chicago, 1968.

————. "Economic Aspects of Rural-Farm Fertility in the United States." *Southern Economic Journal,* forthcoming.

Ghez, Gilbert. "A Model of Life Cycle Consumption Behavior and the Allocation of Time." Ph.D. dissertation, Columbia University, 1970.

Ghez, Gilbert, and Becker, Gary S. "The Allocation of Time and Goods Over Time." Unpublished paper, University of Chicago, 1971.

Gilman, Harry J. "Economic Discrimination and Unemployment." *American Economic Review* 55 (December 1965): 1077–96.

Griliches, Zvi. "The Sources of Measured Productivity Growth: United States Agriculture, 1940–1960." *Journal of Political Economy* 71 (August 1963): 331–46.

————. "Research Expenditures, Education, and the Aggregate Agricultural Production Function." *American Economic Review* 54 (December 1964): 961–74.

————. "Distributed Lags: A Survey." *Econometrica* 35 (July 1967): 16–49.

————. "Capital-Skill Complementarity." *Review of Economics and Statistics* 51 (November 1969): 465–68.

————. "Notes on the Role of Education in Production Functions and Growth Accounting." In *Education, Income, and Human Capital,* W. Lee Hansen (ed.), Studies in Income and Wealth, Vol. 35, pp. 71–115. New York: NBER, 1970.

————. "Education, Income, and Ability." *Journal of Political Economy* 80 (May/June 1972, supplement), forthcoming.

Gronau, Reuben. "The Intrafamily Allocation of Time and the Value of the Housewives' Times." Unpublished research report No. 28, Hebrew University, Jerusalem, June 1971.

Grossman, Michael. "The Demand for Health: A Theoretical and Empirical Investigation." Ph.D. dissertation, Columbia University, 1969.

———. "On the Concept of Health Capital and Demand for Health." Report 7118, Center for Mathematical Studies in Business and Economics, University of Chicago, May 1971; also in *Journal of Political Economy*, 1972, forthcoming.

Hanoch, Giora. "Personal Earnings and Investment in Schooling." Ph.D. dissertation, University of Chicago, 1965.

———. "An Economic Analysis of Earnings and Schooling." *Journal of Human Resources* 2 (Summer 1967): 310–29.

Hansen, W. Lee. "Total and Private Rates of Return to Investment in Schooling." *Journal of Political Economy* 71 (April 1963): 128–40.

———. "Income Redistribution Effects of Higher Education." *American Economic Review* 60 (May 1970): 335–40.

Hansen, W. Lee, and Weisbrod, Burton A. *Benefits, Costs, and Finance of Public Higher Education*. Chicago: Markham, 1969.

———. "The Distribution of Costs and Direct Benefits of Public Higher Education: The Case of California." *Journal of Human Resources* 4 (Spring 1969): 176–91.

———. "A New Approach to Higher Education Finance." In *Financing Higher Education: Alternatives for the Federal Government*, M. D. Orwig (ed.). Iowa City: American College Testing Program, 1971.

Harman, Alvin J. "Fertility and Economic Behavior of Families in the Philippines." Santa Monica: RAND, 1971, in progress.

Hartman, Robert W. *Credit for College: Public Policy for Student Loans*. New York: McGraw-Hill, 1971.

Hause, John C. "Ability and Schooling as Determinants of Lifetime Earnings." *Journal of Political Economy 80* (May/June 1972, supplement), forthcoming.

Heckman, James. "Fertility and Consumption Behavior over the Life Cycle." Ph.D. research in progress, Columbia University, 1971.

Hicks, John. *Capital and Growth*. Oxford: Oxford University Press, 1965.

Hill, C. Russell, and Stafford, Frank P. "The Allocation of Time to Children and Educational Opportunities." Unpublished paper, University of Michigan, 1971.

Hines, F. K.; Tweeten, Luther; and Redfern, J. Martin. "Social and Private Rates of Return to Investment in Schooling, by Race-Sex Groups and Regions." *Journal of Human Resources* 5 (Summer 1970): 318–40.

Hinshaw, Robert; Pyeatt, Patrick; and Habicht, Jean-Pierre. "Environmental Effects on Child Spacing and Population Increase in Highland Guatemala." *Current Anthropology* (April 1972), forthcoming.

Hirschleifer, J. "The Private and Social Value of Information and the Reward to Inventive Activity." *American Economic Review* 61 (September 1971): 561–74.

Husén, Torsten. *Talent, Opportunity, and Career*. Stockholm: Almquist & Wiksell, 1969.

Johnson, Harry G. "A Comment." In *The Residual Factor and Economic Growth*. pp. 219–27. Paris: OECD, 1964.

———. "The Economic Approach to Social Questions." *Economica* 36 (February 1968): 1–21.

———. "Economic Theory and Contemporary Society." *University of Toronto Quarterly* 37 (July 1968): 321–37.

Johnson, Thomas. "Returns from Investment in Human Capital." *American Economic Review* 60 (September 1970): 546–60.

——. "Returns from Investment in Schooling and On-the-Job Training." Ph.D. dissertation, North Carolina State University, Raleigh, 1969.

Jorgenson, D. W., and Griliches, Zvi. "The Explanation of Productivity Change." *Review of Economic Studies* 34 (July 1967): 249–83.

Juster, F. Thomas. "New Directions in National Bureau Research." Paper presented at the joint session of the American Economic Association and the American Statistical Association, Detroit, December 30, 1970.

Kendrick, John W. "Restructuring the National Income Accounts for Investment and Growth Analysis." *Sartryck ur Statistisk Tidskrift* 5, 1966. (See also pp. 9–15 in NBER, *47th Annual Report,* June 1967.)

Kenen, Peter B. "Nature, Capital and Trade." *Journal of Political Economy* 73 (October 1965): 437–60.

——. "Skills, Human Capital, and Comparative Advantage." In *Education, Income, and Human Capital,* W. Lee Hansen (ed.), Studies in Income and Wealth, Vol. 35, pp. 195–230. New York: NBER, 1970.

Kiker, B. F. "The Historical Roots of the Concept of Human Capital," *Journal of Political Economy* 74 (October 1966): 481–99.

——. *The Concept of Human Capital.* Essay in Economics 14. Columbia: Bureau of Business and Economic Research, University of South Carolina, November 1966.

Koehler, J. E. "The Philippine Family Planning Program: Some Suggestions for Dealing with Uncertainties." Santa Monica: RAND, February 1970.

Kothari, V. N. "Disparities in Relative Earnings among Different Countries." *Economic Journal* 80 (September 1970): 605–16.

Krueger, Anne O. "The Economics of Discrimination." *Journal of Political Economy* 71 (October 1963): 481–86.

——. "Factor Endowments and *Per Capita* Income Differences among Countries." *Economic Journal* 78 (September 1968): 641–59.

Kuznets, Simon. "Long-Term Changes." In *Income and Wealth of the United States,* Series II. Cambridge: Bowes and Bowes, 1952.

——. "Economic Growth and Income Inequality." *American Economic Review* 45 (March 1955): 1–28.

——. "Quantitative Aspects of Economic Growth of Nations: Part VIII, Distribution of Income by Size." *Economic Development and Cultural Change* 11, Part 2 (January 1963).

——. *Modern Economic Growth.* New Haven: Yale University Press, 1966.

Kuznets, Simon, assisted by Jenks, Elizabeth. *Capital in the American Economy: Its Formation and Financing.* Princeton: Princeton University Press for NBER, 1961.

Lampman, Robert J. *The Share of Top Wealth-Holders in National Wealth, 1922–1956.* Princeton: Princeton University Press for NBER, 1962.

Lancaster, Kelvin J. "A New Approach to Consumer Theory." *Journal of Political Economy* 74 (April 1966): 132–57.

Landes, William M. "The Economics of Fair Employment Laws." *Journal of Political Economy* 76 (July/August 1968): 507–52.

Leff, Nathaniel H. "Dependency Rates and Savings Rates." *American Economic Review* 59 (December 1969): 886–96.

Leite, Manuela F.; Lynch, Patrick; Sheehan, John; and Vaizey, John. *The Economics of Educational Costing,* Parts I and IIIA. Lisbon: Centro de Economica e Finanças, 1968 and 1969.

Machlup, Fritz. *The Production and Distribution of Knowledge in the United States.* Princeton: Princeton University Press, 1962.

Michael, Robert T. "Dimensions of Household Fertility: An Economic Analysis." Unpublished paper presented at American Statistical Association meetings, Fort Collins, Colo., August 1971.

———. "Education and Fertility." Unpublished paper, NBER, revised 1971.

———. *Effects of Education on Efficiency in Consumption.* New York: NBER, forthcoming.

Miller, Herman P. "Annual and Lifetime Income in Relation to Education, 1939–1959." *American Economic Review* 50 (December 1960): 962–86.

Mincer, Jacob. "A Study of Personal Income Distribution." Ph.D. dissertation, Columbia University, 1957.

———. "Investment in Human Capital and Personal Income Distribution." *Journal of Political Economy* 66 (August 1958): 281–302.

———. "Labor Force Participation of Married Women." In *Aspects of Labor Economics,* H. Gregg Lewis (ed.). Universities–National Bureau Conference Series 14. Princeton: Princeton University Press for NBER, 1962.

———. "On-the-Job Training: Costs, Returns, and Some Implications." *Journal of Political Economy* 70 (October 1962, supplement): 50–79.

———. "Schooling, Age, and Earnings." Preliminary typescript, NBER, 1969.

———. "The Distribution of Labor Incomes: A Survey with Special Reference to the Human Capital Approach." *Journal of Economic Literature* 8 (March 1970): 1–26.

Moynihan, Daniel P. "The Concept of a Public Policy in the 1970s." Unpublished paper delivered at Hendrix College. Washington, D.C.: The White House, April 6, 1970.

Mushkin, Selma J. "Health as an Investment." *Journal of Political Economy* 70 (October 1962, supplement): 129–57.

Myers, Robert G. "Study Abroad and the Migration of Human Resources." Ph.D. dissertation, University of Chicago, 1967.

National Academy of Sciences. *Rapid Population Growth.* Baltimore: Johns Hopkins Press, 1971.

National Education Association. *Financial Status of Public Schools, 1970.* Washington, D.C.: 1970.

Neher, P. A. "Peasants, Procreation, and Pensions." *American Economic Review* 61 (June 1971): 380–89.

Neher, P. A., and Hay, K. A. "Education and Capital Misallocation in a Growing Economy." *Canadian Economic Journal* 6 (August 1968): 609–18.

Nelson, R. R., and Phelps, E. S. "Investment in Humans, Technological Diffusion, and Economic Growth." *American Economic Review* 56 (May 1966): 69–75.

Nerlove, Marc. *The Dynamics of Supply: Estimation of Farmers' Response to Price.* Baltimore: Johns Hopkins Press, 1958.

———. "On Lags in Economic Behavior." Henry Schultz Memorial Lecture before the Econometric Society, Cambridge, September 8, 1970.

Nerlove, Marc, and Schultz, T. Paul. "Love and Life between the Censuses: A Model of Family Decision Making in Puerto Rico, 1950–1960." Santa Monica: RAND, July 1970.

O'Neill, June. "The Effects of Income and Education on Inter-Regional Migration." Ph.D. dissertation, Columbia University, 1969.

————. *Resource Use in Higher Education*. Berkeley: Carnegie Commission on Higher Education, 1971.

Parsons, Donald O. "Specific Human Capital: Layoffs and Quits." Ph.D. dissertation, University of Chicago, 1970.

Pechman, Joseph A. "The Distributional Effects of Public Higher Education in California." *Journal of Human Resources* 5 (Summer 1970): 361–70.

Rasmussen, David William. "The Determinants of the Non-White/White Income Ratio." Ph.D. dissertation, Washington University, St. Louis, 1969.

Razin, Assaf. "Investment in Human Capital and Economic Growth: A Theoretical Study." Ph.D. dissertation, University of Chicago, 1969.

Reischaur, Robert. "Negro Family Relief and Marriage." Ph.D. research in progress, Columbia University, 1971.

Ribich, Thomas I. *Education and Poverty*. Washington, D.C.: Brookings Institution, 1968.

Rosen, Sherwin. "Knowledge, Obsolescence and Income." Unpublished paper, University of Rochester and NBER, November 1970.

Ross, Sue. "The Spacing of Children." Unpublished paper, NBER, 1970.

Ruggles, Nancy, and Ruggles, Richard. *The Design of Economic Accounts*. New York: NBER, 1970.

Sanderson, Warren. "Cohort Analysis to Determine the Probability of Birth." Unpublished paper, NBER, 1970.

Schultz, T. Paul. "The Distribution of Income: Case Study of The Netherlands." Ph.D. dissertation, Massachusetts Institute of Technology, 1965.

————. *Personal Income Distribution Statistics of the United States*. Paper prepared for the Joint Economic Committee of Congress, 1965.

————. "An Economic Model of Family Planning and Fertility." *Journal of Political Economy* 77 (March/April 1969): 153–80.

————. "Effectiveness of Family Planning in Taiwan: A Methodology for Program Evaluation." Santa Monica: RAND, July 1969.

————. "Secular Trends and Cyclical Behavior of Income Distribution in the United States: 1944–1965." In *Six Papers on the Size Distribution of Wealth and Income*, Lee Soltow (ed.). New York: NBER, 1969.

————. "A Framework for Analysis and Its Application to Taiwan's Family Planning Program." Santa Monica: RAND, July 1971.

————. "An Economic Perspective on Population Growth." In *Rapid Population Growth*, Vol. 2, National Academy of Sciences. Baltimore: Johns Hopkins Press, 1971.

Schultz, T. Paul, and Da Vanzo, Julie. "Analysis of Demographic Change in East Pakistan: A Study of Retrospective Survey Data." Santa Monica: RAND, in progress.

Schultz, Theodore W. *The Economic Organization of Agriculture*. New York: McGraw-Hill, 1953.

————. "Reflections on Agricultural Production, Output, and Supply," *Journal of Farm Economics* 38 (August 1958): 748–62.

————. "Education and Economic Growth." In *Social Forces Influencing American Education,* Nelson B. Henry (ed.), pp. 46–86. Chicago: University of Chicago Press, 1961.

————. "Investment in Human Capital." *American Economic Review* 51 (March 1961): 1–17.

————. "Reflections on Investment in Man." *Journal of Political Economy* 70 (October 1962, supplement): 1–8.

————. "Our Welfare State and the Welfare of Farm People." *Social Service Review* 38 (June 1964): 123–29.

————. "Education and Economic Opportunities in Depressed Areas: Implications for Research." In *Problems of Chronically Depressed Rural Areas,* pp. 45–53. Raleigh: Agricultural Policy Institute, North Carolina State University, 1965.

————. *Economic Growth and Agriculture.* New York: McGraw-Hill, 1968.

————. "Resources for Higher Education: An Economist's View." *Journal of Political Economy* 76 (May/June 1968): 327–47.

————. "The Human Capital Approach to Education." In *Economic Factors Affecting the Financing of Education,* Roe L. Johns et al. (eds.), Vol. 2, pp. 29–57. Gainesville, Fla.: National Education Finance Project, 1970.

————. "The Reckoning of Education as Human Capital." In *Education, Income, and Human Capital,* W. Lee Hansen (ed.), pp. 297–306. New York: NBER, 1970.

————. *Investment in Human Capital: The Role of Education and of Research.* New York: Free Press, 1971.

————. "The Optimal Investment in College Instruction: Equity and Efficiency." *Journal of Political Economy* 80 (May/June 1972, supplement), forthcoming.

Schultz, Theodore W. (ed.). "Investment in Human Beings." *Journal of Political Economy* 70 (October 1962, supplement).

Schwartz, Aba. "Migration and Lifetime Earnings in the U.S." Ph.D. dissertation, University of Chicago, 1968.

Scott, Anthony. "The Brain Drain—Is a Human-Capital Approach Justified?" In *Education, Income, and Human Capital,* W. Lee Hansen (ed.), pp. 241–84. New York: NBER, 1970.

Selowsky, M. "Education and Economic Growth: Some International Comparisons." Ph.D. dissertation, University of Chicago, 1967.

Silver, Morris. "Births, Marriages, and Business Cycles in the United States." *Journal of Political Economy* 73 (June 1965): 237–55.

Sjaastad, Larry A. "Income and Migration in the United States." Ph.D. dissertation, University of Chicago, 1961.

————. "The Costs and Returns of Human Migration." *Journal of Political Economy* 70 (October 1962, supplement): 80–93.

Smith, James. "Economic Analysis of Hours of Work." Ph.D. research in progress, University of Chicago, 1971.

Smith, Larry J. "Income and Fertility: An Investment Approach." Ph.D. research in progress, University of Chicago, 1971.

Solomon, Lewis C. "Capital Formation by Expenditures on Formal Education, 1880 and 1890." Ph.D. dissertation, University of Chicago, 1968.

———. "The Relationship between Schooling and Savings Behavior." Unpublished paper, NBER, February 1971.

Soltow, Lee (ed.). *Six Papers on the Size Distribution of Wealth and Income.* New York: Columbia University Press for NBER, 1969.

Stafford, Frank P. "Graduate Student Income and Consumption." Ph.D. dissertation, University of Chicago, 1968.

Stigler, George J. "The Economics of Information." *Journal of Political Economy* 69 (June 1961): 213–25.

———. "Information in the Labor Market." *Journal of Political Economy* 70 (October 1962, supplement): 94–105.

Strumlin, S. G. "The Economic Significance of National Education" (1925). Translated from the Russian and reprinted in E. A. G. Robinson and J. E. Vaizey (eds.), *The Economics of Education,* pp. 276–323. New York: St. Martin's Press, 1966.

Taubman, Paul, and Wales, Terence J. "Mental Ability and Higher Educational Attainment since 1910." Discussion paper 139, University of Pennsylvania, October 1969.

———. "Net Returns to Education." In *50th Annual Report,* pp. 65–66. New York: NBER, 1970.

Telser, Lester. "Some Economic Aspects of College Education." Economics of education research paper 59-5, University of Chicago, 1959.

———. "Some Determinants of the Rates of Return in Manufacturing." Unpublished paper, University of Chicago, 1968.

———. "An Analysis of Turnover in Selected Manufacturing Industries." Unpublished paper, University of Chicago, 1969.

Thurow, Lester C. *Poverty and Discrimination.* Washington, D.C.: Brookings Institution, 1969.

Tobin, James. "Raising the Incomes of the Poor." In *Agenda for the Nation,* Kermit Gordon (ed.). Washington, D.C.: Brookings Institution, 1968.

Tobin, James, and Pugash, James. "The Economics of the Tuition Postponement Option." *Yale Daily News,* February 10, 1971.

U.S. Panel on Educational Innovation. *Educational Opportunity Bank* (Zacharias Committee Report). Washington, D.C.: U.S. Government Printing Office, 1967.

Weisbrod, Burton A., and Karpoff, Peter. "Monetary Returns to College Education, Student Ability, and College Quality." *Review of Economics and Statistics* 50 (November 1968): 491–97.

Weiss, Yoram. "Allocation of Time and Occupational Choice." Ph.D. dissertation, Stanford University, 1968.

Welch, Finis. "Determinants of the Return to Schooling in Rural Farm Areas, 1959." Ph.D. dissertation, University of Chicago, 1966.

———. "Measurement of the Quality of Schooling." *American Economic Review* 56 (May 1966): 379–92.

———. "Labor-Market Discrimination: An Interpretation of Income Differences in the Rural South." *Journal of Political Economy* 75 (June 1967): 225–40.

———. "Linear Synthesis of Skill Distributions." *Journal of Human Resources* 4 (Summer 1969): 311–27.

————. "Education in Production." *Journal of Political Economy* 78 (January/February 1970): 35–59.

West, E. G. "Private Versus Public Education." *Journal of Political Economy* 72 (October 1964): 465–75.

Wilkinson, Maurice. "Swedish and American Fertility Demand Functions." Ph.D. research in progress, Columbia University, 1971.

Willis, Robert J. "A New Approach to the Economic Theory of Fertility Behavior." Unpublished paper, NBER, 1969.

————. "The Economic Determinants of Fertility Behavior." Ph.D. dissertation, University of Washington, 1971.

Willis, Robert J., and Sanderson, Warren. "Economic Models of Fertility: Some Examples and Implications." Paper presented at joint session of American Economic Association and American Statistical Association, Detroit, December 30, 1970.

————. "Is Economics Relevant to Fertility Behavior?" Unpublished paper, NBER, 1971.

Wolfle, Dael. "Economies and Educational Values." In *Higher Education in the U.S.: The Economic Problems,* S. E. Harris (ed.). Cambridge: Harvard University Press, 1960.

Wyon, John B., and Gordon, John E. *The Khanna Study: Population Problems in the Rural Punjab.* Cambridge: Harvard University Press, 1971.

DISCUSSION

Includes comments by Alice M. Rivlin, of the Brookings Institution, and Gerald G. Somers, of the University of Wisconsin, who were the discussants. The recorded oral presentations were edited by, or with the cooperation of, the speakers. Remarks made during the open discussion period are not included.

Alice M. Rivlin: Today, I would like to organize my remarks around three questions: (1) Does research in human resources make any difference to policy makers? (2) How much has it improved policy decisions so far? (3) How can it be made more useful?

First, does research in human capital or human resources matter at all to policy makers? Are they listening? Those of you who have worked in this complex and difficult new area must have occasionally wondered—as you labored over the measurement of foregone earnings or an allowance for ability differences or the choice of the proper discount rate—whether it mattered what you did and whether anyone was ever going to read your work and use it.

I would like to assure you that policy makers *are* listening, perhaps even too hard. They are grasping at shreds of evidence, including the very preliminary results that are coming out of research and seem to offer some guidance for policy decisions.

It is hard to document this judgment, but let me offer three examples of policy decisions that have at least been influenced by research in human capital. First, I believe that the research in human capital and human investment that began to appear in the late 1950's and early 1960's played a role in increasing federal funding for education, health services, manpower training, and other human investment programs, especially for the poor, in the middle 1960's. We probably would have had a war on poverty even if Theodore Schultz and Gary Becker had never written anything, but it might well have been a different kind of war, with far more emphasis on income transfers and less on human investment. The research dramatized the concept of human investment and gave people—even people not familiar with the details of the studies—the basic notion that such investment could pay off. It was this fundamental view of education, training, and health services as investments in people that influenced the thinking, not the rate of return estimates themselves. The strategists of the war on poverty picked up the concept of human investment and jumped, perhaps too quickly, to the conclusion that these investment programs would be most effective in reducing poverty.

A second example, for which there is more evidence, is the disenchantment with human investment programs that took hold of Washington in the late 1960's as a result of disappointing evaluations of such programs as Title I of the Elementary and Secondary Education Act, manpower training, and Headstart. Hope had been high—too high— that human investment would produce dramatic results quickly. When studies did not bear out these hopes, there was an overreaction and a definite shift in federal strategy from investment programs to income transfer programs. There were, of course, other reasons for this shift. The Vietnam War and the threat of inflation were making it necessary to hold back as much as possible on nonmilitary spending. It was very difficult to stem the growth of transfer programs, so a tight lid had to be placed on the investment programs. Nevertheless, one of the contributing factors to this shift in strategy was clearly the evaluation results. Rightly or wrongly, policy makers from the President on down got the impression that human investment programs, especially in education, simply were not working. They decided to hold off on increasing expenditures for these programs until something could be learned about how to get results.

A third example of decisions affected by research in human capital is the impact of recent research on the distributional effects of higher education. The general finding of the researchers that public higher education involved a substantial public subsidy to middle- and upper-income groups should not have been startling or unexpected. Most of us knew that the poor were underrepresented in institutions of higher education, even publicly supported ones, and that, to the extent the poor went to college at all, they went to less costly public institutions, especially to junior colleges. Most of us also knew that the sons and daughters of the well-to-do attended more costly public institutions and stayed there longer. Nevertheless, the work of W. L. Hansen and Burton Weisbrod and others has caused policy makers to stop and think about the way higher education is supported, both at the state and the federal level. State policy makers are questioning whether a low tuition policy is such a good idea if it entails substantial public transfers to people who could afford to pay for higher education and would probably go to college even if the subsidy were less. It is now respectable to argue that raising tuition in public institutions and using the money for student aid to the really poor would be preferable on distributional grounds to current policy.

At the federal level, these research results have influenced, or at least reinforced, the recent shift in federal strategy from institutional aid to student aid. The results have supported the contention that aiding students is a more effective way to ensure equality of opportunity in higher education than giving construction money or other institutional aid to colleges and universities. All political decisions are complicated, of course, but the research evidence on distributional effects of present state support for higher education has certainly been among the many factors which have influenced both this administration and the last one *not* to propose a program of general federal aid to higher education institutions.

My conclusion is, fellow researchers on human capital: Policy makers *are* listening. They are eager for help. They may even pick up your results and run with them before you think they are good enough to be used as a basis for action.

To the second question, "How much help has the research in human capital been?" my answer is "only a little." The work has thrown some light on the distribution of human capital. It is clear that human capital is quite unequally distributed, although not as unequally as non-human capital. The research in human capital has also been useful in predicting how changes in major types of human investment might be expected to affect economic growth and the distribution of income. It has not, however, been very useful in telling us specifically what we ought to be doing—how to invest in human capital most effectively. The microeconomic side, the production function, if you will, has not been greatly elucidated. Research has not yet told us much about how to organize a health system effectively, how to produce education efficiently, how best to retrain workers, how to promote migration, and so forth.

It is my view that these micro decisions will be crucial decisions of the 1970's. Public concern seems likely to focus more and more on the problem of how to produce effective public services. Research, if it is to be useful, must focus on these production problems as well.

Gerald G. Somers: My remarks will relate primarily to the manpower area, only one area of investment in human beings. I was interested in

Professor Schultz's stress on supply and demand in research on human capital and the implication that the demand for research and information is very great. At my university of late one comes to wonder whether the demand for our research is really that large, since our legislature and regents insist that professors should spend more time in the classroom. The pressure is growing, not only at Wisconsin but also at Michigan and a number of other universities, to reduce the research time of professors. With this happening, we have to be more concerned than ever with the allocation of scarce resources. We may not be able to do as much research as in the past. We have to be increasingly careful that research on human capital should be an investment with a positive rate of return.

The key question that came to my mind as I read through Ted Schultz's excellent paper (and here's where I argue a bit with Alice) is why the human capital tool of analysis, honed to a fine point in the 1960's, did not have a greater impact on manpower policy. Data and the computer became more readily available. All of the forces were right for a tremendous influence on the development of manpower policy, which also burgeoned in that decade. The thrusts in federal manpower policy that began in 1961–62 and evolved in a cumulative fashion as the decade progressed were closely related to the concept of human capital. I am not denying that the discussion of investments in human beings may have been connected with the general idea of training people, or of giving them basic education courses, or of helping them to realize their full potential through vocational education. But what interests me is that the manpower policy changes that occurred appeared to be coincidental. In the 1960's there was a manpower policy revolution, with continuing revisions and additions to manpower programs. However, the policy changes did not seem to reflect the theoretical and empirical work on investment in human capital, on the cost-benefit analysis, on the analysis of the rates of return to various kinds of training, and the returns to migration, mobility, or labor-market information. The question is why? This was a golden opportunity. At a time when Congress was eager to expand programs in this area and new policies were being forged, when we had a growing number of cost-benefit analyses in the manpower field, why did the analyses of investments in human capital fail to influence the policy makers?

For example, the shift in emphasis from institutional to on-the-job training began in the Johnson administration; and there was a major concentration in the Nixon administration on the NAB-JOBS program (the National Alliance of Businessmen's training in the business sector), a program of subsidizing private employers. Employers are urged to hire and train the disadvantaged worker, and, if the job remains filled, the employer gets $3,000. Presumably this is compensation for taking on someone whose marginal productivity is below the going wage, and there may be a sound economic basis for such a program. But why did manpower policy take this turn at this particular time? I can't recall anything in the cost-benefit analyses which would call for such a change in direction. The writing of Mincer showed a positive return to on-the-job training, but it was a broad concept of on-the-job training, including "learning by doing," with data derived neither directly from cost records of employers nor directly from opportunity costs of the trainees. This was an imaginative approach, given the lack of data. But it did not tell us that we ought to give employers a subsidy to hire the disadvantaged. Some might place a contrary interpretation on Mincer's results: that employers should not require a government subsidy because of the big payoff of on-the-job training. As it turned out, with higher unemployment in 1970–71, the NAB-JOBS funds were not fully used. Employers did not even want the subsidy. The times were such that the shift from institutional to on-the-job training proved to be not a very wise departure for manpower policy. Surely some of the cost-benefit analyses should have provided more guidance for the policy makers on this question.

Now the present major thrust of the Nixon administration is the Manpower Revenue Sharing Bill. Manpower funds are to be allocated to the states and to the localities which are to be given substantial freedom in planning and executing the manpower programs. I see nothing in the investment analyses of human capital or in the cost-benefit studies that leads us to that conclusion. In fact, on the basis of evidence, one might well conclude that this is a questionable policy at the present time. Regional and local authorities are no more able than federal agencies to run manpower programs. I agree with Alice that there has been a checkered career for manpower programs in the federal agencies; but the evaluations do not show that we would have done better if we had passed all of the manpower funds to the local communities to run the programs as they saw fit. Some proposed legislation is based on the current WIN program—Work Incentive Program for welfare recipients. What do we know through cost-benefit analyses, from research on investment in human beings, that suggests that it would be wise to insist that mothers on welfare take training programs? What leads us to believe that this would pay off in terms of equity or efficiency? Some are being trained for low-level service jobs and others are being financed for a university education leading to teaching degrees. Given the possible family needs for the services of welfare mothers at home, the first type of training is a questionable type of investment. And given the growing surplus of teachers, one cannot be sure that the latter is the best investment. If we look at it purely as a consumption effect, most of us would take pleasure in a welfare mother's achievement of a bachelor's degree and a teaching certificate. However, is this a wise investment in human capital from the standpoints of employment and earnings? The evaluative research provides no proof that it is. Whereas Alice seemed to be impressed with the big impact research on human capital has had on policy formation, I am impressed with the small effect it has had on the variations in manpower policies and on the adoption of new programs.

The question raised by a reading of the Schultz paper is why research on human capital has had so little effect on the changes in manpower policy. One easy conclusion is that "it's all a matter of politics." If the administration decides that manpower programs should be concentrated in the private sector, this will be the direction of legislative change even when there is no evidence that the rate of return on private training of the disadvantaged is greater than that on public training. Similarly, if the administration has a political preference for revenue sharing and decentralization in the realm of social policy, manpower proposals will follow in this direction regardless of the conclusions reached by the analysts of human capital investments.

However, it is too easy to simply dismiss the limited role of human capital analyses by saying that manpower policies reflect the political climate. As Alice Rivlin has pointed out, congressmen are not oblivious to research findings and policy evaluations. If the facts and conclusions are presented clearly and persuasively, the analysts can have some impact on changes in manpower programs and other investments in human resources.

One is led to the conclusion that it is not only in the political system but in ourselves where we have failed to have a greater impact on the modes of investment in human capital. The deficiencies may well be in the theory of human capital and in its application to manpower policy. Professor Schultz has raised the question of the narrowness of the human capital concept. But he has not fully pursued the implications of that narrowness for the development of social policy. He has noted that human capital is an economic concept, dealing with costs and benefits essentially in economic terms. He suggests that efforts should be made to broaden the social context of human capital analysis. In my view, the concept must be broadened if human capital analysis is to influence congressmen, administrators, and manpower policy.

In suggestions for further research, Professor Schultz might have gone much further in urging more research on procedures for expanding the concept of human capital. It is really a task for the theorists of human capital as well as for the research investigators, and I urge more theoretical work along these lines upon our chairman, Gary Becker, as well as upon those engaged in empirical studies.

Congressmen and administrators cannot be fully convinced by research on human capital when the findings are couched in terms of monetary benefits, while the needs of their constituents may be primarily social or psychological in nature. Professor Schultz has noted that investments in human capital lead to a stream of earnings and/or satisfactions. More must be done to incorporate measures of satisfactions and dissatisfactions in the costs and benefits of manpower programs. This requires a cooperative effort of economists, psychologists, and sociologists. The major advances in both the theory and practical application of investment in human capital are likely to be along these lines in the next few years. There have already been some good beginnings. There have already been some measures of satisfaction utilized as dependent and independent variables in regression analyses of manpower programs. These variables require further refinement. The recent analyses of leisure and other nonmarket activities as they relate to the investment in human resources will also help to broaden the concept of human capital and make it a more useful tool of analysis.

The second reason for the limited impact of human capital analysis on manpower policy derives from the heterogeneous nature of the investment in human capital, and in our failure to recognize the significance of this heterogeneity. As we all know, the weakness of some of the growth models lies in the fact that they usually aggregate all of the capital investments, assuming that the rates of return to all capital investments are equal. As Professor Schultz has pointed out, it is the very inequality in the rates of return to different kinds of capital investment which is the essence of economic growth. In many cases, the variation in rates of return to different investments in human capital is also the essence of the growth of human beings. We often tend to forget this point as we evaluate the investment in human capital as an aggregate with a single rate of return. Or, more frequently, we have separate evaluations of the investment in a training program, in a vocational education program, in a labor mobility program, or in public education. There has been only a limited effort to analyze the interaction of these various investments when they impinge on the same human being. We know very little about the results of the interaction of manpower training and subsidized mobility, two programs in which the federal government has invested funds. We know little about the results of the interaction of preschool education, basic public education, and adult education. Nor do we know much about the relationship of these types of education to vocational training. Under what circumstances does an investment in basic literacy training for adults give a positive rate of return, both economic and noneconomic? Is it true, as one or two recent studies seem to show, that such literacy training for adults, when not accompanied by occupational training, provides little or no benefit for the recipient?

To what extent is one type of investment in human beings cancelled out by another? For example, do government subsidies to move workers from depressed rural areas to city employment opportunities make it more difficult to convince employers to hire and train the existing ghetto residents of that city? Professor Schultz has asked why the government hasn't done more to guide migration. Why has there not been greater public investment of this type? Perhaps if there were more research on the interaction of the investment in mobility with other types of public investment, such as those in training and education, a more convincing case could be made for relocation subsidies. Limited research has shown that employers in one large Midwestern city prefer the white Anglo-Saxons brought in from the rural areas to the minority disadvantaged whose employment the government is trying to promote. Other research has shown that the combined retraining and relocation of workers from depressed areas has a higher rate of return than either retraining or relocation carried out separately. Just as in the combination of basic literacy instruction and occupational training, certain combinations of investment produce a much higher rate of return than separate investments.

Why have we not had a greater impact on the development of manpower policy? The answer may well lie in the need for a theoretical broadening of the concept of human capital and for further empirical research on the interaction of the varying investments in human beings. If policy makers are to be influenced by the analysts of human capital, the analysts must make a more convincing case.

INDEX